The
Exit
Roadmap

The insider's guide to selling
your business profitably

Chris
Spratling

R^ethink

First published in Great Britain in 2025
by Rethink Press (www.rethinkpress.com)

Contents

Introduction

When you've ridden the roller coaster of growing a business, nothing should come as a surprise, but the work involved in *selling* your business can certainly throw up many surprises along the way. The exit journey often starts with excitement – the anticipation of crowning your life's work, that moment when you finally get to enjoy the fruits of your labour. But, after a while, if you're not prepared for the reality of what's involved, it has the potential to descend into confusion, stress and disappointment.

The unfortunate truth is that few business owners achieve the sale they want. Sadly, more than 50% of people who sell their companies are dissatisfied with the outcome and, according to Forbes, 75% even regret doing it at all, mainly on the grounds of how little they received.[1,2] These are scary statistics and I'm sure you don't want to become one of them.

Here are some more numbers. Brokers and corporate finance houses estimate that only 20% of businesses available for sale each year are sold within a twelve-month period, and that some 65% of businesses on the market never sell at all.[3] In many cases, their owners had unrealistic expectations, didn't really understand what was involved, and often failed to enlist the right support to help them navigate the process. The result was that they had no choice but to step back and let someone else run their business, or close it down and forego the rewards of all those years of blood, sweat and toil.

Selling your business successfully won't take care of itself; you need to know what to do before, during and after the transaction if you're to secure a successful outcome. You may well have a long-standing and trusted accountant who you're convinced can provide you with all the help and advice you need, but my experience tells me that, in most cases, a traditional compliance-led accountant is rarely enough. It's no coincidence that most successful deals are achieved by entrepreneurs

1   Prince, RA and Bowen Jr, JJ, *The Enrichment Report* (Gold Family Wealth, 2017), https://growfl.com/why-are-50-of-business-owners -unhappy-after-they-sell-their-company, accessed 10 February 2025
2   De Pau, L, 'When Should You Decide To Sell Your Business?', *Forbes* (1 August 2024), www.forbes.com/sites/liendepau/2024/08/01 /when-should-you-decide-to-sell-your-business, accessed 10 February 2025
3   Debussy, A, *BizBuySell Insight Report* (BizBuySell, no date), www .bizbuysell.com/insight-report, accessed 13 February 2025

who recognise the importance of building a strong deal team of experienced professionals that includes the likes of a corporate finance expert, a broker, a tax planner, a commercial law firm and a wealth manager.

Then there's the knowledge and information you need to steer your way through the often-treacherous waters that make up the business sale journey. If you don't understand the various steps in the process and why they're important, you'll not be able to make the right decisions along the way.

You can only sell your company once, so getting it right from the 'get go' is essential. That means there's a lot more to do up front than you might assume. While individual acquirers have differing objectives, they all want to make an investment that generates a return as quickly and reliably as possible. To satisfy their aims you may need to make some fundamental changes to your operations, the way you lead and manage your teams, and even to your underlying business model before you put your company up for sale.

Then there's the sale itself. You need to market your business in a way that catches the eyes of potential buyers, before deciding between the various offers you receive. This can involve embroiling yourself in negotiations over lengthy legal documents with opaque language. It's hard to know what to do for the best, and yet it's invariably one of the most important transactions that you'll ever make.

The good news is that, now you have this book, you won't be alone on your journey. It's a step-by-step, no-nonsense roadmap to everything that's involved in selling a business, showing you what you can do to maximise the value of your company when you sell. With it, you stand a high chance of achieving a price that reflects all the work you've put into building your firm. Without it, you run the risk of selling at a price that significantly undervalues its true worth.

I wrote this book because I've spent the last thirty years buying and selling companies myself, as well as advising people who are selling their own. During this time, sadly, I've seen the same mistakes made over and over again. It frustrates me that I can't help everyone personally, so this is my attempt to guide you through the process. In it, you'll learn everything I teach my own clients so that you, too, can sell your company smoothly and successfully.

In Part One, you'll learn how to prepare for sale success. This involves discovering things like:

- What you need to know about your personal finances before you sell
- The ten drivers of business value and the impact they have on your sale price
- Who your ideal buyer might be and what they seek in an acquisition
- When is the right time to sell and how long it will take
- How much your company is really worth

In Part Two, we'll explore the sale itself. You'll learn essentials such as:

- How best to put your business on the market
- How to navigate the offers you receive and to negotiate the best price and terms
- Ways to smooth and speed up your buyer's due diligence process
- The steps you need to take to complete the sale
- How to affect a handover that makes life as easy as possible

At the end of each chapter, you'll see summary points and, because I'm a practical person, some chapters also finish with suggested action points. Please use these to help you put what you've learned into practice.

I'm sure you don't need me to tell you this, but the decision to sell your business is more than just a financial one. It also has profound personal and professional implications for the next chapter of your life, and for that of your employees. Don't be like the 48% of entrepreneurs who have no exit plan, or the 58% of business owners who've never had their company formally valued.[4] Start preparing your business for sale by embarking on Chapter 1 today.

---

4   Wilson, T, '48% Of Business Owners Who Want To Sell Have No Exit Strategy' (Brooks Holdings, 2018), https://kbrooksholding.com/2018/02/48-business-owners-want-sell-no-exit-strategy, accessed 10 February 2025

PART ONE

PREPARE FOR SALE SUCCESS

1

What Does Success Look Like? Navigating The Decision To Sell

Four years ago, one of my clients, James, took his business to market. Unbeknownst to us, his long-term competitor had decided to go to market at almost exactly the same time. On a positive note, both businesses sold successfully, but the story got most interesting after they'd both transitioned to new ownership. What James and I then learned was that both companies had had a similar turnover and adjusted earnings before interest, taxes, depreciation and amortisation (EBITDAs), and yet – to our delight – James' had sold for almost 50% more than his competitor's. Why? Because of the thorough preparation he'd put into maximising the value of his business before bringing it to market and into the sale itself.

James understood that selling a business is a huge step to take, not only financially, but also personally and professionally. The amount they sell for, and the terms they accept, can often shape the rest of the seller's life. And yet, for such an important decision, I'm always surprised by how few business owners put much thought into why they want to sell, how much for, and what factors they should consider when they embark on the process of selling. Research has shown that, out of all business owners who say they expect to sell their business at some point, fewer than half have created any sort of exit plan.[5] This is a concern, because deciding to sell your business marks the beginning of a new chapter in your life. Plan it well and you'll maximise the value of your company, minimise disruptions when it's sold, and reach your personal goals in the way you want. Fail to plan and you may achieve none of these things.

Minimising disruption is an under-appreciated benefit of planning. If your exit is well planned, you'll be able to keep the business going during the transition from one owner to another. You'll be able to anticipate problems, create contingency plans, and communicate with all your stakeholders in a way that brings them on board. This will, in turn, reduce any negative impact on your employees, customers and suppliers alike. If one of your motivations for selling is to leave a legacy and make sure that your staff are well looked after, this is critically important.

5   Wilson, T, '48% Of Business Owners Who Want To Sell Have No Exit Strategy' (Brooks Holdings, 2018), https://kbrooksholding.com/2018 /02/48-business-owners-want-sell-no-exit-strategy, accessed 10 February 2025

Maybe you have a clear view of what your business is worth, know exactly how potential buyers will value it, when you'll put it on the market, and what you'll spend the proceeds of a successful sale on. You're also sure about what kind of offer you want, and you've thought about who will run your company when you're gone. If so, congratulations – you're a rare founder. But even if this is the case, it's still important to re-examine your expectations to make sure that they're realistic, and to create plans that will help you to achieve your goal. The good news is that, with some forward thinking, you can be one of the outliers who's able to optimise the value of your business and achieve a successful sale.

The phrase 'start with the end in mind' is one that I use constantly. If you know what you want to achieve by selling, it makes all the other decisions you make along the way much easier. That's why, in this chapter, we'll explore your personal goals and motivations, delve into the intricacies of your decision to sell, and broach the subject of valuing your business. We also look at the factors you need to consider when you decide to sell, and what makes for a successful sale.

What's your motivation?

If I've learned anything from my years of coaching entrepreneurs through the selling process, it's that everyone's different. Each person has their own reason for putting their company on the market, and each has their own vision of what life will be like on the other side. Some of those reasons aren't ones that they would necessarily care to share openly, which is why I'm privileged to be part of their journey. While there's a wide variety of motivations, they tend to fall into four overall camps:

- Financial security
- Change of lifestyle
- Strategic shifts in the marketplace
- Personal fulfilment

I'm going to explore each in turn, with the aim of helping you home in on what's most important to you. This is important because if you don't know why you want to sell, how will you make sure that you achieve what you want? There are many ways to dispose of a business, each suited to different motivations, and if you don't identify yours, you could well become one of the majority of sellers out there who are dissatisfied with their post-sale results. If you know what you want, on the other hand, you stand a much better chance of getting the result you're after.

Financial security

The big one. If you're like many entrepreneurs, this may well be the most significant factor behind your decision to sell: to secure your future financially, whether that be for your retirement or for setting up another business. It's interesting that, according to organisations like The

Federation of Small Businesses, the typical SME business owner has between 80% and 90% of their overall wealth tied up in their company.[6] This is huge. If this is you, unlocking the value of your company can give you the financial cushion you need to move into the next phase of your life with confidence.

The security you gain from selling is naturally bound up with how much you sell for. I've often found that business owners are unsure about how to value their companies, or, even if they are, they aren't realistic about the numbers. Sometimes their businesses are worth less than they think and sometimes more, which is why I'll introduce the subject of valuing your business in a moment.

Change of lifestyle

You may want more time to do your own thing, such as pursue a passion, travel the world, or just relax in the garden. Maybe you dream of moving to another country or a different part of the UK, where you wouldn't be able to run your business in its current form. If you're coming up to retirement age, selling potentially gives you the opportunity to do this, and if you're younger and have ambitions to make your mark in other ways, you'll have the funds to set you on your way.

---

6   Kowalski, C, 'Understanding Exit Planning', The Exit Planning Blog (9 January 2023), https://blog.exit-planning-institute.org /understanding-exit-planning-epi-and-maus-partnership, accessed 13 February 2025

Wanting more free time can sometimes be down to health issues, either your own or those of your family. One of my clients, Bruce, decided to sell up so he could look after his wife who'd been recently diagnosed with Alzheimer's. It wasn't easy for him to give up working ('If you rest, you rust' is how he put it), but he was determined to enjoy the time he had left with her while they were still able to do things together.

Strategic shifts in the marketplace

Being a business owner has probably taught you that adapting to new market trends and technological changes is essential if you're to keep surviving and growing. But what if you see storm clouds gathering on the horizon that you don't like the look of? It might make sense to make a strategic exit before the going gets tough. If, on the other hand, the changes you see on the horizon are positive, you may feel they're more easily exploited by a new business owner who's better positioned to capitalise on them than you are.

Personal fulfilment

Selling your business can also be a hugely satisfying way of realising the rewards after years of effort, giving you a profound sense of achievement and paving the way for new adventures at the same time. Why not give yourself the pleasure of seeing your efforts bear fruit in the form of a sale?

Another way of gaining personal fulfilment from

selling your company is to pass it on within your family. A surprisingly high number (88%) of business owners expect to do this, but the fact is that few manage to do so. According to SCORE, only 30% of companies ever pass to the next generation, 12% to the third, and a mere 3% to the fourth.[7] It's also important to be realistic about whether your family is willing and capable of running your business. One of my clients, Edward, owns a furniture company with a £5 million turnover. The company generates a healthy £1.5 million a year at a net-profit level, but despite this, he wants to retire because he feels that he's reached an age where there's more to life than work. His son is currently the Managing Director and could in theory take over the company, but Edward doesn't believe that he has the skills to run it on his own. Given the probable value of the business, it's also highly unlikely that his son could raise the funds to buy it. Edward is wrestling with what to do, but at least he's thinking about it now and building the various options into his plans.

Whether your decision to sell is prompted by plans to retire, changes in your marketplace, a desire to lead a different kind of life, or simply a yearning to see the results of your years of hard work in your bank account, knowing your 'why' is crucial. That's because if you understand what you want to achieve at the end of the

---

7   Score, 'Infographic: The Family Business – Successes And Obstacles'
     (2018), www.score.org/resource/infographic/infographic-family
     -business%E2%80%94successes-and-obstacles, accessed 10 February
     2025

process, you'll be in a good position to make the right decisions to help you get there.

Valuing your business

A few years ago, I was approached by a lovely couple, Robert and Susan, who ran an online business selling premium, chemical-free paints. The trend towards environmentally friendly decorating, particularly among people with money to spend, had caused their company to blossom. It was an extremely profitable and robust business which they wanted to sell so that they could retire, and they'd been referred to our consultancy by their financial advisor. So far so good, but the problem was that, when I dug into what they thought their business was worth versus what they needed to retire on, it quickly became apparent that the numbers didn't quite add up. Not least because, while Robert and Susan were in their mid-sixties, they had a daughter in her forties with a severe disability who required expensive round-the-clock care. If they couldn't pay for this, the alternative was for her to be taken into local authority care, which they couldn't countenance.

As much as I would have loved to help them sell, I couldn't see how it could ever be at a value that would enable them to look after their daughter for the rest of her life. Instead, I suggested that they let me help them grow their business so they could hire someone to run it and release time for themselves. This they did, and have recently been able to step back and do things they enjoy using the income that comes in.

This is a stark example of having a specific objective for selling but not understanding how much is needed to fund a lifestyle. From my experience, 70% of sellers have no idea what post-tax income they'll require to live on after the sale. They don't know what's in their pension, how much it will yield in the form of an annuity or other recurring income, and whether that matches up to what they currently spend plus the extra things they want to do – such as travel the world or help out their children. Do you?

While they may think that they know what their business is worth, it's often based on anecdotal evidence or comparisons with similar businesses that have sold, but which in reality are very different under the hood. This is usually down to a misunderstanding about how valuations work. According to Forbes, 58% of small- and medium-sized businesses have never been formally valued, which can lead their owners to have unrealistic expectations about what they're going to receive when they sell.[8] As I have said, sometimes their companies are worth more than they think, and sometimes less, but either way, it's not a good place to start when they're planning the rest of their lives.

I detail how to value your business in Chapter 6, but for now, it's worth bearing in mind that a company 'like yours' can't be valued simply by applying a multiple

---

8   Hannon, K, 'How Women Entrepreneurs Should Prepare To Sell A Business', *Forbes* (24 May 2018), www.forbes.com/sites/nextavenue /2018/05/24/how-women-entrepreneurs-should-prepare-to-sell -a-business, accessed 13 February 2025

or putting it alongside one that looks the same from the outside. That's too subjective. For instance, companies located in different parts of the country may well sell for different amounts because they have differing regional customer bases, and it's not easy to know what behind-the-scenes work those businesses might have been doing that has had a significant influence on their sale price.

What makes for a successful sale?

Close your eyes for a moment and allow yourself the indulgence of picturing your dream future a few months after the sale. What are you doing and how much money do you have to enjoy it with? Are you still involved with your business or are you out of it entirely? Do you care about who's running it now, and if so, do you like the way they're going about it? Thinking about these things will move you closer to deciding what kind of deal you want – in other words, what a successful sale looks like for you.

I've come to the conclusion that successful deals are a blend of:

- The price you achieve
- The structure and timing of the offer
- The buyer's plans for your business and whether they sit comfortably with you

To help you see what I mean, let's look at an example scenario with two alternative options. Let's say you put your business up for sale and the total offer you're given is £5 million. This is structured into an immediate payment of £2.5 million, with the rest split into three equal payments over the following three years.

In Option One, these payments are dependent on the future performance of the business. If it doesn't hit the agreed targets, the instalments you're paid are reduced accordingly. Alternatively, if the business exceeds the targets, it may well yield a higher overall price for the business. How would you feel about that? Is it what you want?

In Option Two, you receive the offer above, but instead of having to hit performance-related targets, you're paid instalments regardless of performance. While this sounds more reliable, it has its pros and cons. If you miss your targets, you'll have the benefit of receiving the payments regardless, but if you overshoot them, you may well end up foregoing a higher overall payout.

That's why the deal you strike needs to be dependent on both your market growth and on how confident you are in your business' ability to become more profitable in the future. To complicate matters, you might also feel strongly about what kind of buyer you want to take over your business, especially if you have employees whom you want to see well looked after. If this is important to you, it can make a difference to how you approach the sale.

Personal preparation

The rest of the first section of this book is devoted to how you can ready your business for being put on the market. But I suggest that you don't only plan for your business – make it about you as well. It's easy to be so focused on the sale that you forget to think about what you're going to do afterwards. You might assume you can work that out when the time comes, and maybe you will, but it never does any harm to prepare for life after the sale. Dare to dream.

Think about the impact your newfound wealth will have on you and your family. While you might assume this will be positive, it isn't always the case. Ahmed was a business owner I worked with who sold 60% of his business to his management team six years ago. His vision had always been to buy a new house, and he had an exact picture in his mind of what it would look like and where it would be. Sure enough, as soon as he sold his share of the company, he moved out of the small, terraced place he'd been living in for twenty years and into a £1.5 million new-build on a large plot of land. You'd think that would be a happy ending, but five years down the line there's still ongoing tension between him and his wife because she continues to find the transition to their newfound wealth difficult.

Another thing to think about is what you'll do with acres of free time. While your other half may have been begging you to sell so they can spend more time with you, now you're at home more, you might both find the space a bit crowded. Planning how you're going to live a more comfortable lifestyle will help to reduce tensions, and minimise regrets, after the event.

When you know why you want to sell, have a realistic idea of what your business is worth, have envisioned what kind of sale you want it to be, and how you're going to live after the sale, you will have maximised your chances of success. You understand what success means for you, and the planning you've done will give you the best opportunity to make it a positive and fulfilling experience.

In the next chapter, we'll explore more about whether you're ready to sell. In the process, you'll learn about the ten drivers of business value and how your business matches up to them.

SUMMARY POINTS

- Planning ahead increases the chances that you'll sell your business for an amount you're happy with.
- When you know why you want to sell, you're likely to achieve the outcome that's right for you.
- Valuing your company isn't something that you can estimate based on comparisons with others and guesswork.
- Think about what you want to do with your extra time and money now, rather than later.

ACTION POINTS

- Get clear on your big reason for selling your business; if you need to, talk to colleagues, friends, family, or an advisor.
- Work out how much you need to sell for in order to live the life you want after the sale; this will involve reviewing your pension and other financial arrangements.
- Think about what involvement, if any, you want to have in your business after it's sold.

2
Are You Sale-Ready?
The Ten Drivers Of
Business Value

When you're thinking about selling your business, it can be surprising to discover that, while the business may be yours, the decision about when to sell it isn't always yours to make. At any given moment, you could be approached by someone with an amazing 'now or never' offer, or your market might go through an unexpected shift which makes it the ideal time to put your company up for sale, or you may have a sudden change in personal circumstances and need to liquidate your assets. Or something else might happen entirely. Whatever your situation, you have to be 'sale-ready' when the moment comes. If you're not, you might have to choose between passing on a great opportunity because your business isn't in the right place, or being pulled into a sale that undervalues it.

Being sale-ready means having a business that's

positioned to maximise its attractiveness to a potential acquirer. Over the years, I've gained a deep insight into what buyers want when they look for a company, and I've come to the conclusion that there are several factors they take into account. I call these the ten drivers of business value, and they are:

1. A history of strong growth

2. The potential to scale up

3. Recurring or contracted revenues

4. Positive market positioning and points of difference

5. Low reliance on key staff

6. Low reliance on key customers

7. Low reliance on you as the owner

8. Healthy working capital

9. High customer loyalty

10. Protected intellectual property

In this chapter, I'll explain these drivers in more depth and give you strategic tips for how you can make your business sale-ready by focusing on each of them in turn. Some of the drivers merit a whole book in themselves, so my tips are just that – top-line advice for what you can do. They give you a steer in the right direction so that you can explore the relevant areas in more detail if you need to.

As you read through, you'll see that these drivers are based on two things: boosting your company's value and reducing the level of risk for a buyer. That's because buyers are looking for businesses that will provide a decent return on their investment *and* don't contain any hidden problems that will return to bite them after the transaction. Imagine the total price for your company being a bucket, and every time you fulfil one of the drivers, some water goes in, while every time you present a risk, some water comes out. It's worth remembering that, if an acquirer is in a position to pay you a seven- or eight-figure sum, they have choices about what to do with that money. They could simply put it in the bank and earn interest on it if they wanted to, so if they're going to buy your business, they have to be confident that it will generate a significant enough return relative to the risk they're taking.

While you're learning about the ten drivers, you may be asking yourself how sale-ready your own business is. You can discover this by filling in our online survey here: www.chalkhillblue.org/exitreadiness-survey It will help you to avoid being overwhelmed by steering you in the direction of the most important drivers to focus on when you're readying your company for sale.

Driver 1: A history of strong growth

Nothing says 'buy me before someone else does' like a business that has a track record of profitable, consistent growth. This not only shows potential acquirers that they're taking on a robust company that can deliver a return on their investment, but it also gives them confidence that it's been well run. It paints you as a high-return and low-risk proposition, because for a buyer, there's an attractive level of predictability and stability in a business that's grown steadily over the years. You've obviously been able to generate reliable revenue streams, foster good customer relationships, keep your business relevant to its market, and establish effective operational processes. In other words, you've done a great job.

This reduces any uncertainty a buyer might have and makes it likely that they'll be willing to pay a premium. Valuation multiples, such as price-to-earnings and price-to-sales, tend to be higher for companies with strong growth trajectories, and this can lead to a better sale price for you.

Finally, there's another benefit to having a solid growth record: you make your company attractive to a broader range of buyers, including strategic acquirers, private equity firms and institutional investors. You're fishing in a larger pond than if you're reliant on a single contact or interested party, which in turn increases the chances of a competitive sale process, invariably leading to higher offers.

Tips for creating strong growth

Through working with many businesses to help them enhance their attractiveness to buyers, I've come to the conclusion that there are five key financial metrics to focus on when it comes to growth:

- Revenue growth rate
- Profit margins
- EBITDA
- Cash flow
- Customer lifetime value

Without exception, I've never met a company owner who didn't see a benefit from investing time and energy into developing strategies to enhance these metrics before a sale. Here's a top-line guide to what you can do:

- **Revenue growth rate.** The rate your revenue is growing is an indicator of your business' ability to generate higher sales in the future. You can accelerate this by expanding your customer base, introducing new products or services, entering new markets, and boosting your sales and marketing efforts.

- **Profit margins.** Buyers see your profit margins as evidence of how efficiently you manage your costs and optimise your pricing. You can increase your margins by streamlining your operations, keeping your expenses under control, negotiating more favourable terms with suppliers, and pricing your products or services in a way that reflects their value to your customers.

- **EBITDA.** This is earnings before interest, taxes, depreciation and amortisation. The higher your EBITDA, the more you look like a business that has good earning potential and is well run. You can raise your EBITDA by increasing your revenue, reducing your operating expenses, enhancing your productivity and thinking carefully about what you spend money on.

- **Cash flow.** Having a strong cash flow is essential for ensuring that your business stays liquid and is financially stable. It also convinces a buyer that, after they've bought your company, they'll be able to meet its financial obligations and fund its growth in the future. I'll give you more advice on cash flow in the 'healthy working capital' driver.

- **Customer lifetime value.** You may have seen this described as CLV – it's the total revenue or profit that each of your customers generates over the course of their relationship with your business. If you've created a high CLV over the years, it shows that you can generate sustainable revenue from long-term customer relationships. You can maximise your CLV by driving repeat business through targeted marketing campaigns and personalised customer experiences, and by putting in place customer retention strategies.

Driver 2: The potential to scale up

It's worth remembering that, when you sell your business, it's the end of the journey for you but it's just the beginning for your acquirer. They're buying the company's future performance, so they're more interested than you might assume in whether your company has expansion opportunities built in. These could take the form of scalable models, innovative products or untapped markets.

However, it's not enough for you to be confident that your company has potential for expansion, you also have to paint a clear picture of *how* it can be scaled up over the next three to five years. That's why drawing up a roadmap for the future is essential – it's clear evidence that your business is poised for growth, which will give you stronger bargaining power during negotiations.

You can also see that, for a buyer, being able to envisage how your company could grow makes it feel as if the purchase is a less risky proposition. They can see how a purchase would complement their existing operations or expand their market reach, or enable them to leverage synergies to create more value. In this way, a well-defined scale-up strategy plan gives them the reassurance that your company will fit into their broader strategic vision, which in turn increases the likelihood that you'll gain a higher price at sale.

Tips for creating scale-up potential

Again, experience has taught me that scaling a business requires a different mindset to simply growing a business. Business owners who manage to scale in a significant way have certain traits in common: they're able to get to the heart of a problem quickly, they have exceptional decision-making skills, and they can juggle the strategic and operational goals of their company based on their knowledge of how to take advantage of opportunities. For me, scaling is about doing more with less.

I'm very much of the view that entrepreneurs typically scale their businesses through four key focus areas, namely:

- Marketing

- People

- Technology

- Investment

Consequently, a buyer is likely to want to see a strategic scale-up plan that details how your business will, at the very least, ensure it's able to deliver successfully in the following areas:

- **Acquire new customers and retain existing ones.**
  Scaling a business involves both acquiring new customers and retaining existing ones. You can recruit new customers through well-targeted advertising, and retain existing customers by offering an exceptional service and implementing loyalty programmes.

- **Move into new markets or launch new products.**
  If you're to grow, you need to make extra products to sell or find new markets to sell into – or both. This involves doing your market research, identifying untapped opportunities, and assessing what your competitors are doing. Whether you plan to expand geographically, into adjacent

markets, or by diversifying your product range, this will position you to grow in the future.

- **Build automated processes and invest in technical infrastructure.** You can't scale without increasing your operational efficiency, and the best way to do that is by investing in technology. It will help you to create systems for managing your various business processes, thereby streamlining your operations and standardising your procedures. You can, for instance, scale up your workforce by using cloud-based technologies and flexible workspaces. When you're not wasting time doing things manually and in a bespoke way, you free up resources to scale.

- **Develop strategic partnerships.** One way of scaling is to collaborate with strategic partners, as it gives you access to new resources and markets. These partnerships could be with complementary businesses, suppliers or distributors – anyone who can help you to expand your reach. Alliances can also open up opportunities for sharing marketing and product-development costs, and for pooling your knowledge so that you can be more innovative. All this leads to quicker and more efficient growth than if you were to go it alone.

Driver 3: Recurring or contracted revenues

If your business has customers who are locked in through long-term contracts, or who have signed up for repeat orders via subscriptions, this helps to alleviate a buyer's concern that, once they take over the business, revenue could drop off a cliff because you're not running it anymore. In fact, these kinds of income streams are something of a holy grail for buyers for this reason alone.

A great example of this from a buyer's perspective is a household cleaning products business that my wife and I bought out of administration a few years ago, and which we still own today. In its fourteen years of existence, it had never made a profit, but in our first year of ownership the profits reached £250,000. The way we achieved that was to create a subscription model, and then systematise the business from top to bottom so as to eradicate all labour-intensive activities and enhance the overall customer experience. This allowed us to reduce the headcount from sixteen to four, while ploughing some of the operational savings into enhanced digital marketing activities. This significantly increased our sales. Today, with only a couple of hours a week input from us, we earn £20–30,000 profit from it a month.

Buyers also know that recurring and contracted revenues mean they have to expend fewer resources on sales and marketing, as repeat customers cost less to retain than recruiting new ones. They can allocate their funds to growing the business rather than to replacing customers who've made one-off purchases.

Moreover, businesses with predictable and recurring revenue streams are often seen as resilient when it comes to market fluctuations. This makes it easier for a buyer to justify paying a higher price, as they can forecast future cash flows with confidence. They also know that repeat income likely equals loyal and satisfied customers, another advantage for you when it comes to negotiating a sales price, as it points to a strong brand and a competitive advantage in the marketplace.

Finally, recurring or contracted revenues give a buyer an advantage when it comes to scaling your business in the future. If you have a predictable income, this lays a solid foundation for extending into new markets, adding new products or services, and expanding the business to cater for increased demand. We're back to the benefits of having a business that's capable of strong growth, which was our second driver of business value.

Tips for creating recurring or contracted revenues

Just about every buyer is looking for an acquisition that can deliver stable and sustainable revenue streams for the foreseeable future. And just about any corporate finance firm will tell you that, if you can achieve this *before* putting your business on the market, it will increase your valuation at sale. To this end, there are a few elements that you can put in place to set up recurring revenues:

- **Subscription-based models.** Offering your products or services on a subscription basis is the key way of establishing predictable revenues and creating long-term customer relationships. Once you've transitioned to a subscription model, you can put in place subscription tiers, value-added services and incentives for your customers to pay annually (thereby locking them in for longer).

- **Long-term contracts and service agreements with customers.** These give you stability and predictability and can take the form of discounts or incentives for customers to commit to extended contracts, or to renew existing ones. As part of this strategy, it's obviously important to make sure that you offer incredible service, so your customers want to stay with you.

- **Up-selling and cross-selling to existing customers.** By identifying extra customer needs and then offering complementary products or services to satisfy them, you can increase your CLV and your incremental revenue at the same time. Ways to do this include personalised marketing campaigns, making smart use of customer data, and providing targeted recommendations to customers.

- **Membership programmes and loyalty schemes.** Offering exclusive benefits, discounts or rewards encourages your customers to keep coming back. It also creates a sense of belonging and strengthens their loyalty to your business. An added benefit is that you can use these schemes as a way of generating recurring revenue by charging subscription fees, so not only do they increase customer retention, but they also bring in regular income in their own right.

- **Value-added services and maintenance contracts.** Providing ongoing support, maintenance or training services alongside your core products and services can give you additional recurring revenue streams. On top of that, they increase customer satisfaction and encourage long-term relationships.

Driver 4: Positive market positioning and points of difference

You'll usually find significant competition in any industry, so if your business stands out, it's a draw for a buyer. Having a strong, differentiated brand shows you have a loyal customer base that's attracted to your points of difference, which in turn almost certainly reduces the perceived risk for your acquirer. It also means that the business can potentially charge a premium; when customers feel an emotional connection with a business, they're less likely to jump ship just to save a bit of money. This points to profitable revenues now and in the future.

Having a strong market positioning can also indicate that you've adapted to changes in your marketplace over time. For a buyer, this may well be seen as evidence of your company being resilient to shifts in the business landscape that would threaten a weaker brand. Buyers can see that yours is a company with a stable revenue stream and sustainable growth potential, all because of the solid branding it's based on. This allows them to envisage themselves introducing complementary products or services, expanding geographically, or targeting new market segments – possibly in ways that they're better positioned to do than you are.

Just as with your growth plans, however, it's important for you to articulate your points of difference. Buyers might not understand the intricacies of your market as well as you do and may not appreciate your unique value proposition and why it matters. When you present a clear and compelling statement about how you're better and different, you not only find yourself more attractive to acquirers through standing out, but you also raise the value of your business when it comes to selling.

Tips for creating a positive market positioning and points of difference

I've seen first-hand the immense commercial benefits of investing in a strong market positioning before selling. Here are some ways you can do this for yourself:

- **Brand identity and differentiation.** It's essential to stand out in your market. First, carry out market research to understand your customers' preferences, the competitive landscape and emerging trends. This will help you to identify your unique selling proposition (USP). Then refine your brand messaging and visual identity to clearly communicate your positioning.

- **Product or service innovation.** Investing in continuous innovation in terms of features, functionalities or offerings can help you to differentiate yourself and attract interest from potential acquirers, but only if what you develop meets your customers' needs or resolves their pain points; if it's innovation for the sake of it, it won't help you.

- **Segmentation and targeted marketing.** Analysing your customers' demographics, behaviours and preferences to create segments enables you to tailor your marketing messages and campaigns to high-value groups. Through this, you can strengthen your market positioning by directing your resources at the most worthwhile targets and position your business as the best choice for their needs.

- **Customer experience and service excellence.** Providing personalised, responsive and memorable experiences at every point in your customers' buying journey is fundamental to creating a strong market position. You want your customers to love everything about you and to recommend you to their friends. This involves investing in employee training and creating a customer support system that consistently delivers great experiences.

Driver 5: Low reliance on key staff

As part of your buyer's due diligence process, they'll invariably delve into how work gets done in your company, and to what extent it's dependent upon a few key individuals. The last thing they want is to pay a lot of money for a business only for one or two important staff members to say to themselves, 'You know what? The boss has gone and I'm not sure what it's going to be like working here now. I'm ready for a change, so I'm off too.' This isn't ideal in any situation, but if your company is over-reliant for its day-to-day running on these people, it presents a huge risk for your buyer. The same employees may have specialised knowledge that's critical to the business' success or be the only people who've ever liaised with certain important customers. If they leave (or are even absent for a while), clients might look elsewhere, operations could crumble, and new business may drop off. It could be a real headache for the new owner and jeopardise the continuity they'll be wanting to keep going.

Buyers will also be aware that being over-reliant on certain people will make it harder for them to grow the business in the future. It's no good having a company that has the potential to scale if there's a lack of flexibility in its staffing arrangements. When employees are restricted by their responsibilities, it's difficult to expand into new markets or make the most of opportunities to grow. It's also a sign of poor management and leadership if specific people in the company have total responsibility for some areas, as this can stifle creativity, collaboration and innovation. Many buyers won't want to take on a business that needs a human resources overhaul.

Of course, dedicated employees are a benefit, so there's no harm in emphasising their value, but only if you can also show that your company's success doesn't rest disproportionately in their hands. This is an area that's primarily about reducing risk for your buyer, so the more you can show that reliance on key staff is nothing for them to be concerned about, the higher the price you can sell for.

Tips for reducing reliance on key staff

This area is often a weakness for small businesses, so it's important that you protect yourself (and your future acquirer) from the risks associated with it. Here are my top strategies for avoiding over-reliance on key staff:

- **Promote cross-training and knowledge-sharing.** Your goal here is to make sure that critical skills and knowledge are spread around as many employees as possible. You can do this by giving them opportunities to do tasks outside of their primary roles and encouraging them to share their expertise with others. The outcome of this will be a more versatile and adaptable workforce.

- **Document your processes and procedures.** You should encourage your employees to document their workflows, best practices, and key insights to make sure that your business isn't reliant on certain individuals. When you have everything written down, it ensures that your company's operational knowledge is available to everyone. This can take the form of manuals, standard operating procedures and knowledge banks which hold critical information.

- **Empower middle management.** When you delegate decision-making authority to those lower down the hierarchy, this reduces your dependence on key people at the top. You can invest in leadership development programmes, mentoring and coaching to prepare your middle managers for these responsibilities. The result will be that, by sharing power across multiple layers of your organisation, you decentralise control and reduce the risks associated with a senior person taking all the relevant knowledge and skills with them when they leave.

- **Recruit and develop talent.** You need a pipeline of skilled people ready to take on new roles when someone departs. This involves identifying your high-potential employees from within, as well as having recruitment strategies to spot people externally.

- **Draw up redundancy and contingency plans.** These help you to reduce disruption when key people leave, especially when it's unexpected. This is where the cross-training I mentioned earlier comes in, but you can also create backup roles, a bit like having an understudy in a play.

Driver 6: Low reliance on key customers

This driver is about ensuring that you have a diversity of income streams. If a buyer discovers that a large proportion of your revenue comes from a small number of customers, it will often ring alarm bells for them. By 'large proportion', I mean more than 10% coming from one customer, or 80% from the top eight to ten customers. That's because, if one of those customers were to take their business elsewhere (or even go bust themselves), it could blow a huge hole in your company's future performance. This is something that could easily happen after the sale, especially if the reason they leave is because they have a close business relationship with a key member of staff who leaves (see driver 5) or with the owner (see driver 7).

There are times when this rule can be relaxed. For instance, one of my clients who's preparing to sell his business receives half of his revenue from one customer. But that customer actually represents a dozen other customers who buy through the same entity. There's still a risk for an acquirer, but it's partly offset by the fact that those dozen customers could, and probably would if they needed to, buy direct from my client's business in the future.

Being over-reliant on a small number of customers could also be seen as a sign that your business isn't well managed. Maybe you've coasted along with some comfortable and loyal relationships without making the effort to diversify and gain new business. This could also limit your ability to negotiate better terms with those customers, and a buyer may well conclude that your company would need a lot of work to make it robust and viable.

Tips for reducing reliance on key customers

Just as with over-reliance on key members of staff, it's important to show acquirers that your business isn't vulnerable to one or two important customers leaving. Here are the key ways of doing this:

- **Diversify your customer base.** No surprise here. Are there new market segments you can target? Different industries? Further geographic regions? Put in place some targeted marketing to bring your products or services to these new markets by discovering where the people in them spend time and joining them there. One of my clients, who had a strong customer base in the automotive sector but was over-reliant on it, realised that he could expand his seating product into airlines – a much more profitable industry for the type of innovation he sold.

- **Develop strategic partnerships.** Creating alliances with other businesses which are complementary to yours can open avenues for gaining new customers. These collaborations can take the form of co-marketing, cross-promotions and joint sales efforts, and will put you in front of people whose attention you might otherwise find it hard to gain.

- **Expand your product or service ranges.** When you have products or services that appeal to a diverse range of customers, it helps you to expand your reach. Ask yourself whether, with some market research, you might have the opportunity to develop something new for a customer base that you've not served before. It could be a totally new product line or a variation on what you already sell.

- **Tie in your customers.** If you can incentivise your key customers to commit themselves to long-term contracts, you'll mitigate the risk of them leaving. These contracts might be based on them staying with you for a certain amount of time, or spending a specific amount of money, or both. Of course, you need to offer exceptional service as well, to ensure that they don't feel the need to go elsewhere.

- **Be more effective with your sales and marketing.** It might be that you need to be cleverer about who you target and how. By investing in sales training and lead-generation campaigns, refining your marketing messaging, and making the best use of the marketing channels available, you can improve your conversion rates. This will help you to diversify your customer base so that you're not reliant on too few players.

Driver 7: Low reliance on you as the owner

If all your customer relationships, supplier relationships and internal relationships centre on you as the business owner, an acquirer may well see this as another significant risk. To discover whether this is the case, they'll ask questions such as: do you have a sales director with their own sales team, or do you handle all the sales yourself? Is the success of your customer relationships down to their satisfaction with your company, or is it because they've known you personally for a long time? Do you have people who run the day-to-day operations of the business, or are you heavily involved yourself? Are the terms you receive from suppliers preferential because they're documented in a contract, or because you've negotiated them informally based on your personal relationship with them?

That's invariably why a buyer wants to see that you have a management team which is as invested in the business and as capable of running it as you are – in effect, it's what they're buying. It's also why you need to reduce your company's dependence on you well before you bring your business to market. Even if you're comfortable with the idea of staying on to run the company for a year or two after you sell, its over-reliance on you will typically reduce the value of your business considerably.

It also doesn't look good from a performance perspective if you're heavily involved in the day-to-day running of your business. While any buyer will acknowledge that you, as the owner, have played a significant part in the growth of your company, they'll also know that if you're the one making all the decisions, you're a limiting factor in how easy it will be to expand it. An owner who's perceived as controlling will find it impossible to foster the culture of innovation and autonomy that attracts talent and enables a company to flourish.

So, how reliant is your business on you? A good test is to ask yourself whether you could go away for six months and come back to a business that's just as well run as it was when you left, if not better. If you know from experience that you can't even take a two-week holiday without answering (or worse, making) work-related calls on your sun lounger, you probably have some changes to make.

Tips for reducing reliance on you as the owner

Enabling your business to run independently without you is both a practical and emotional journey. It can be hard to let go of the reins, so here are some strategies for making the transition:

- **Develop a strong management team.** This is critical. By hiring skilled people, promoting internal talent, and giving leadership development opportunities, you can cultivate a team that's capable of driving your business forward without you. This should include a managing director to oversee the senior team. And it's not enough to have the right people in place; you also need to empower them to make independent decisions.

- **Document your processes and procedures.** Just as with an over-reliance on key employees, you need to document all your personal processes, procedures and best practices. While you're about it, you can standardise your workflows so that other people can follow them; this will make your organisation more efficient. Frameworks such as ISO are useful for this.

- **Put systems in place.** If you're involved with the day-to-day operations of your company, implementing some systems that don't need your input can be a big help. Technical solutions, such as enterprise resource planning and customer relationship management software, are good examples. These take away control from you and make information accessible to those who need it.

- **Engage advisory boards and external consultants**. These bring independent expertise and guidance into your business, reducing its reliance on you for strategic decision-making. Not only that, but you'll find that having external input gives you valuable insights and perspectives.

Driver 8: Healthy working capital

A buyer wants to be confident that your business can generate enough cash for its daily operations, while also generating a surplus that can be turned into profit or invested in growing the company. This is why the working capital assessments that they make during the financial due diligence process have an impact on how much they're prepared to pay for your company.

Businesses are typically bought on a cash-free, debt-free basis, less normalised working capital. We'll go into the intricacies of this in a later chapter, but as a summary, when a business sale price is agreed, the buyer is effectively putting a value on the company while also evaluating the cost of running it.

It's easiest to explain using an example. Let's imagine that I'm a buyer and I value your company at £2 million. In theory, I'm therefore offering to pay you £2 million for it. However, let's also imagine that you have cash in your business bank account to the value of £200,000. As I'm buying your business on a cash-free basis, I'll give you pound-for-pound what you have in that account. This increases my offer to £2.2 million:

Value of business	£2,000,000
Plus cash in bank	£200,000
Cash-free offer	**£2,200,000**

However, you also have £100,000 worth of debt, made up of outstanding loans plus yet-to-be-paid corporation tax, VAT and PAYE. As I'm buying your business on a debt-free basis, this reduces my offer to £2.1 million:

Value of business	£2,000,000
Plus cash in bank	£200,000
Less debt	- £100,000
Debt-free offer	**£2,100,000**

Here's where working capital comes in. Let's say that your customers typically pay you on credit terms of two months, and let's also say that your running costs amount to £50,000 a month. That means I would need two months' worth of running costs as working capital, which works out at £100,000. This is the amount that I will expect you to leave behind in the business, and which reduces my offer yet again, to £2 million:

Value of business	£2,000,000
Plus cash in bank	£200,000
Less debt	- £100,000
Less working capital	- £100,000
Debt-free offer	**£2,000,000**

This is a highly simplistic example but you can see how, if you were to reduce your company's working capital requirement, you can gain a higher offer. Halving it, for instance, would net you an extra £50,000. Equally, generating more cash means that your buyer won't have to fund as much of the working capital themselves, leaving more to spend on the acquisition itself. This is usually the area in which there's most negotiation when it comes to agreeing a final sale price. It's also one that reveals much about your company's financial discipline, resistance to market downturns and its stability, which is another reason to get it right.

Tips for creating healthy working capital

Given the importance of building a strong working capital position before you sell, it's worth spending time on these strategies for improving it:

- **Optimise your inventory management.** By putting in place just-in-time purchasing systems, forecasting demand more accurately, and negotiating longer payment terms with your suppliers, you can free up working capital. That way, at any moment in time, less of your money is in your suppliers' bank accounts and more of it in your own.

- **Reduce payment times to you.** When you shorten your accounts receivable collection cycle, you're paid more quickly. This improves your working capital position because money comes in from customers faster than it goes out to suppliers. You can do this by having an efficient invoicing process, offering discounts for early payment and establishing clear credit policies. Technology, such as automated invoicing systems and electronic payment options, can also help to make accounts receivable more streamlined.

- **Increase payment times to your suppliers.** This is the flip side of the above. Consider negotiating extended payment terms, taking advantage of early payment discounts and optimising your payment schedules. These all help to align your accounts payable outflows with your cash inflows.

- **Reduce your operating expenses.** Are there any day-to-day running costs that you could cut back on or eliminate? This reduces the demand on your working capital. Options include carrying out a comprehensive review of your expenses, re-negotiating contracts with suppliers and improving your operational efficiency by streamlining processes, reducing waste and using technology to reduce your overheads.

- **Sell your noncore assets.** Could you sell any surplus stock, equipment or property assets? What about leasing excess capacity in your office space or selling off any nonstrategic business units? The proceeds would give you a cash boost, thereby improving your working capital position. You could use this to increase your bank balance or to reduce your debts.

Driver 9: High customer loyalty

One of the typical concerns of a buyer is that your customers will defect to a competitor after the purchase. Having a high level of customer loyalty, and evidence to prove it, helps to mitigate this risk.

It's widely accepted that the best and most common measure of customer loyalty is what's called the net promoter score (NPS). This is a metric that's become increasingly popular with acquirers, particularly private equity firms. So, how do you create an NPS? In essence, you send your customers regular surveys in which you ask a standard question: 'On a scale of 1 to 10, how likely are you to recommend us?' Scores of 9 or 10 are considered positive, 7 or 8 ambivalent, and 6 to 1 negative. To calculate your overall score, you add up the positive scores as a percentage of the whole, remove the negative ones, and end up with a number which represents your NPS. For example, if 60% of your respondents are promoters and 10% are detractors, your NPS would be 60 − 10 = 50.

Having a high NPS doesn't only reassure your buyer that your customers will stay with your company after the sale, it's also evidence of your brand value. You've clearly worked hard to create a business that offers an excellent product or service that people are happy to buy and recommend, creating a high customer lifetime value in the process. That means your business is resilient, competitive and capable of growth. What's more, buyers know that, as the saying goes, what gets measured gets done. So, the simple fact that you're measuring your NPS before you put your business up for sale shows that you take customer satisfaction and loyalty seriously.

Although each of the ten drivers of business value interrelates with one another, high customer loyalty is one that encapsulates almost all of them. When customers are happy to buy from you repeatedly, you're able to grow and scale. You're likely to have recurring revenue, a positive market positioning, and healthy working capital, and the risks associated with being over-dependent on key individuals or customers dissipate. That's why companies which measure their NPS and work on strategies to grow it usually achieve high valuations when they sell.

Tips for creating high customer loyalty

Given that your NPS is such a firm indicator of how viable and robust your business is, it's worth spending time on these strategies for increasing your customer loyalty:

- **Enhance your customer experience across all touch points.** Carry out a review of all your customer touch points, from initial contact to post-purchase support. Then make sure that your employees are trained to give outstanding service at each stage. By consistently exceeding your customers' expectations, you can raise your NPS.

- **Seek and act on customer feedback.** As part of the above, you can put in place feedback mechanisms for customers to tell you what they think, so that you have the information to act on their concerns. You can use surveys, interviews and online reviews to gather data, which will give you the ability to spot trends and uncover pain points.

- **Personalise your communications and services.** People want to be treated as individuals. By segmenting your customers based on whatever criteria are relevant to your brand, you can tailor your offerings to their preferences and needs. Ways of doing this include using data analytics and customer relationship management systems to track interactions and anticipate needs.

- **Empower your employees.** When you give your front-line staff the autonomy and training they need to solve customer problems effectively, it makes a positive impact on those customers. It's important to reward employees who do a good job of this, as having a customer-centric culture is key to raising your NPS.

- **Track your NPS metrics.** If your aim is to create a higher NPS, it goes without saying that you need to measure it regularly and monitor its performance. So, set goals for improving it and track the key performance indicators (KPIs) related to customer satisfaction and loyalty. The wonderful thing about measuring your NPS is that you'll find yourself putting initiatives in place to improve it. Then, as if by magic, your customers will become more loyal, they'll spend more money with you, and your business will achieve the growth we talked about in the first two drivers of business value.

Driver 10: Protected intellectual property

Intellectual property (IP) includes patents, copyright, trademarks and design protection. For the purposes of this final driver of business value, it also includes customer data, because data is proprietary information that's legally yours to exploit in the same way that IP is. Buyers are often willing to pay a premium for companies with strong IP portfolios, as they see them as having a competitive advantage over those which haven't protected their assets.

To understand this, let's imagine you've developed a product that's foundational to your business' success. If you haven't patented the design, there's nothing to stop a competitor creating their own identical product, thereby piggy backing on your hard work. They could undercut you and even force you out of the market, because your lack of protection makes you vulnerable. If, however, you have a patent in place, you're able to differentiate yourself in the marketplace and compete more confidently, as customers know that they can't buy the same thing elsewhere. Just as importantly from the perspective of selling your business, acquirers will be reassured that they're purchasing a valuable asset – one that they might even be able to sell on to someone else one day.

The same goes for innovations that you've developed for internal use. Suppose you hire a consultancy to code some software that allows you to operate more efficiently than your competitors. If you protect it, it's yours, and the consultancy can't sell it to anyone else.

That means other companies would have to spend time and money replicating it from scratch. You can even put the IP on your balance sheet as a way of increasing the health and wealth of your business, which could lead to a higher valuation when you come to sell.

Another reason acquirers like to see protected IP in a business is that it provides a platform for future growth. Patents and trademarks with broad market appeal can unlock additional revenue streams when you sell your products into new markets. As an additional benefit, protected IP reduces the risk that a buyer might be taking on a company that's vulnerable to legal challenges from competitors, which gives them comfort and certainty.

Tips for protecting your intellectual property

Protecting IP is often the difference between a business achieving an average and an industry-leading (sometimes eye-watering) valuation. I'm amazed at how often I come across business owners who overlook IP protection because they wrongly believe that their company doesn't have any IP. When you think about it, your company almost certainly has its own unique brand identity, one or more website domains, and a company logo – at the very least. There's always something to protect. So please don't overlook the obvious and miss out on a chance to derive value from what you already have. Here are my top strategies for doing this:

- **Identify and protect your valuable IP assets.**
  First, carry out an audit to identify all your IP

assets, including patents, trademarks, copyrights and trade secrets. Next, protect them through registration, licensing agreements, confidentiality agreements and other legal mechanisms.

- **Monetise your IP assets.** You can look into exploiting your protected IP through licensing agreements, joint ventures, or even by selling it outright to entities who are interested in using your technology, brands or content. It's a way of unlocking hidden value in your business, which makes you more attractive to a buyer.

- **Actively manage your IP portfolio.** An IP portfolio is something that should be actively managed so as to maximise its value. It's best to prioritise investments in research, development and innovation if you want to generate new assets that allow you to grow and expand. This will help you to stay relevant in the marketplace.

- **Use your IP assets for competitive advantage.** Make sure that you promote the USPs that your IP gives you when it comes to marketing your products or services. Through this, you position yourself as an industry leader and increase the value of your business.

- **Mitigate risks and ensure compliance.** It's important, as part of your active IP portfolio management, to keep on top of relevant laws, regulations and industry standards. You also need to make sure that you identify any IP infringements that affect your business and put in place protective measures against them. This will boost your credibility with potential buyers.

Maximising sale value

It's worth noting that for each of the ten drivers of business value, by reducing risk you also increase value, and vice versa. For instance, while it might at first seem that the main benefit of reducing your company's reliance on you as the owner is that it removes risk for a buyer, that's not the whole story. It also increases value, because by building a management team that can run it without you, you make your company more innovative and resilient. This stimulates your business to grow, and with scale comes a higher price at sale.

Of course, the price could be reduced if a large proportion of your sales were to come from one customer, or if you haven't protected your IP, which is why you can never generalise about companies of similar sizes receiving similar multiples in their valuations. But it does go to show that all ten of these drivers of business value interact with one another and should never be seen in isolation.

This has been a long but important chapter. So many of the business owners who come to me for advice about selling their companies are unaware of the goldmine that sits under their noses if they were to implement the strategies that I've given. So many of them are at risk of losing huge amounts of money in a low value sale because they don't see the risks that their company presents to a buyer. Now that you know what to do, you're positioned to make a lot more from your business than you otherwise would have.

In the following chapter, we'll look at the different types of buyers you might consider for your business. This will help you to take the next steps towards getting your company ready for sale.

SUMMARY POINTS

- Gaining the highest possible sale price for your company involves both increasing its value and reducing the risk it presents to a buyer.
- There are ten drivers of business value, which, if you maximise the potential of each, can make an enormous difference to the money you receive at sale.
- It's therefore worth spending a considerable amount of time implementing the strategies for each driver before you put your business up for sale.

ACTION POINTS

- Gather your senior leadership team and go through each driver of business value in turn. Rate your business from 1 to 10 for each or use my online survey tool here: www.chalkhillblue .org/exitreadiness-survey.
- Create a prioritised list of actions based on the strategic tips that I've given you for each driver.

- Draw up a plan for implementing them. This is a project that might take months or even years, but by doing it, you create an estimated timescale for putting your business up for sale.

3
Who's Your Buyer? The Five Types Of Business Acquirer

Who do you want to buy your business? You may have a clear idea about the person or company. Maybe it's another entrepreneur like yourself – someone who will carry on your good work and treat your staff as you do. Perhaps it's a venture capital fund with deep pockets. Or maybe it's one of your suppliers or competitors who sees your business as being complementary to their own.

Whatever assumptions you've made, the answer to the question is ideally not just one buyer, but as many as possible. Of course, only one acquirer will walk away with your company, but there's no single type of entity who 'should' buy you out. In fact, you want a wide variety of people to show an interest – as many as fifteen to twenty – so that you stand the best chance of receiving a handful of serious offers. Because it's competition between buyers that raises the acquisition price.

For that reason, I encourage you to broaden your horizons when it comes to envisaging your eventual buyer. In the same way as you've probably been selling your product or service to customers from different walks of life, you should expect your business to attract varying types of acquirer. And just as you should know your audience when it comes to promoting your products, so you should know your audience when it comes to marketing your business.

When you promote your brand, you ask yourself questions like:

- Who are my customers?
- What's their motivation for buying from us?
- Where are they located?
- What do they want and need?
- Why might we want their attention?
- Why might we not want their attention?
- What are they prepared to pay?

Through asking and answering these questions, you can gain a deep understanding of those people or organisations so that your marketing efforts bear fruit. As any marketing expert will tell you, simply promoting your products to 'everyone' never works.

In addition to the above, when you're selling your company, you need to ask a few extra questions, this time not about your customers but about your potential acquirers:

- How are they structured?
- Why do they want to buy my business?
- What do they intend to do with it after the acquisition?
- How will they decide how much to pay?
- What will they prioritise when they carry out due diligence?
- How does my business fit with their strategic goals?

When you've answered these questions, you'll be well placed to make the strategic changes in your business that will attract the kind of buyers you want. You'll also be able to tailor the marketing of your organisation in a way that makes clear why they should be interested in you. This goes for buyers whom you *don't* want to attract, too. For instance, if you want to discourage individual entrepreneurs from the process, you can lay down conditions that they'll be unlikely to meet, such as that the majority of the transaction must be funded from their cash reserves.

We'll explore how to align your business to your favoured buyer types, and how to market your business at sale, in later chapters, but for now, it's important to realise that if you don't know who you want to attract in the first place, you can't do any of that effectively. For this reason, we'll spend the rest of this chapter analysing the different types of buyers.

The five types of business buyer

Given that your aim is to create competition by attracting multiple, credible offers from more than one type of buyer, you need to understand the differences between the various buyer types. This helps you to avoid wasting time marketing yourself to the wrong people (those whose goals don't align with your company's strengths, or who don't have deep enough pockets), and to concentrate your efforts in the most profitable way. When you have a number of offers from acquirers who have both the interest and the funds to buy you out, you have the upper hand in the sale negotiations.

Here are the five types of business buyer:

1. The individual buyer
2. The strategic buyer
3. The financial buyer
4. The family office
5. The internal buyer

Let's look at each in turn. By the time we've finished, you'll be able to decide what kind of buyer, or buyers, you want to focus your attention on.

The individual buyer

This type of buyer is someone much like you or me: an entrepreneur who might, or might not, have run their own company before and is looking to take the plunge by acquiring a business. Often a first-timer, they're inexperienced in the buying process, but that doesn't mean you should write them off as being naive. They've probably worked in business for years, either in the corporate world or through running their own company, and are likely to be financially astute.

A good example of an individual buyer is one of our clients, Sarah. A few years ago, we helped her to sell her training business, but after some months travelling the world, she's now back home and ready to invest what's left of the proceeds in a new challenge. As such, she has her eye on a particular company that she thinks has potential: a waste-disposal firm. Of course, she doesn't know much about waste disposal, but she does know how to grow a business successfully – she's proved that already. For her, this is about having a fresh adventure and making a deal that will net her a decent return on her investment.

Their motivations

The individual buyer tends to be on the lookout for a small business that they can easily take up as an owner-operator – one that appeals to their personal interests or specialised knowledge of a sector. The purchase is usually part of their long-term goal to give themselves a healthy annual income through acquiring an established business and growing it over several years.

Their requirements

They'll be detailed in their due diligence and scrutiny of your business and will be keen to know what assets you have, especially in terms of infrastructure, property, inventory and people. They're after a company with a great team of employees who can facilitate a smooth transition, and which has enough working capital to make it viable. Having possibly run a company like yours before, the individual buyer knows that people are critical to an enterprise's success.

Things to think about

Selling to the individual buyer can be rewarding because you have a clear picture of who you're handing over your precious company to. They're personally invested in building it into something greater and might even be someone you know already. However, they can sometimes be inexperienced, which means that they don't always understand the sale process, and they will invariably lack the funds that a larger acquirer might have. They can offset this by opening up the deal to third-party financing options or through staged payments, should you agree to it, but you do have to accept the inherent limitations of the individual buyer in this area.

The strategic buyer

The strategic buyer comes in the form of a company that wants to expand or consolidate its businesses by acquiring another one. Unlike the individual buyer, the strategic buyer is rarely a first-time entrepreneur but a seasoned veteran who already runs a company; sometimes they've already bought (and sold) several times over. They'll acquire your business and eventually assimilate it into their own, where it will supplement their core operations and boost their profits.

Their motivations

The strategic buyer aims to give themselves an advantage by bringing your business into their fold, so it follows that their operations should be in some way complementary to your own. They might be one step above or below you in the value chain, such as being a supplier or a customer. They may even be a competitor. The synergies from the purchase are designed to boost their bottom line by making them more competitive, increasing their influence, helping them to branch out into new markets, or strengthening their resilience.

You can see examples of strategic purchases all over the tech world when firms spot potential competitors in their infancy and snap them up to give themselves a foothold in a complementary area. Examples are Google buying YouTube in 2006, and Facebook acquiring Instagram for $1 billion in 2012 when it only had thirteen employees, then picking up WhatsApp for $19 billion in 2014. A more down-to-earth example is one of our current clients, a timber importer. They're currently being acquired by one of their largest customers, a fencing contractor. The synergies are obvious; the fencing firm gains the profit margin that they've previously paid as part of their timber purchases, and also has a secure supply of a material that can sometimes be hard to source.

Their requirements

Although strategic buyers are looking to boost their profits through an acquisition, their first consideration when choosing a business to buy isn't purely financial. They're mostly concerned with whether your company is a strategic fit with theirs in a way that will help them to compete more effectively. That's not to say that they wouldn't like a business that will add to their bottom line quickly and efficiently *as well as* being a great strategic fit – who wouldn't? – but the driver is stronger than the prospect of instant profit. They also want a company that's versatile enough to integrate into their own ecosystem as seamlessly as possible.

Things to think about

Because the strategic buyer focuses their evaluation on how well your business fits with their core operations, it's possible to strike a good deal with them even if you don't have the most impressive financial record. The secret is to show how your business systems and assets are perfectly aligned with their short- and long-term goals. If you're able to do that, you may gain a premium price for your business, and for that reason, selling to a strategic buyer can be one of the most rewarding exit options.

The flip side of the above, though, is that, because the strategic buyer looks to integrate your business with theirs, the brand you've worked so hard to develop might end up being swallowed into the larger whole. Likewise for some of your employees, who could find their services surplus to requirements in the new entity. You have to be willing to accept these potential outcomes if you sell to a strategic buyer.

The financial buyer

Financial buyers can take various forms:

- Private equity firms
- Hedge funds
- Venture capital firms
- High-net-worth individuals

Like the strategic buyer, the financial buyer is almost always an established business rather than a person; even if they're a high-net-worth individual, they operate through a company. But while the strategic buyer is focused on how your business might fit into their own, the financial buyer is more concerned about your financial track record.

As an example, we recently sold an accountancy business at five times adjusted EBITDA to a larger regional accountancy firm that was backed by private equity. This larger business had also bought others of a similar structure and value, and wanted to put all their acquisitions together with the aim of selling for a seven to nine times multiple. In their case, they weren't explicitly looking to add value to those businesses individually, but to derive profit from scaling up.

Their motivations

Whatever form they take, the financial buyer has one aim: to grow their earnings and profits through buying other businesses. They're not so much interested in buying your business because of its expertise as they are in generating maximum returns on their investment.

Their requirements

Because of the above, the financial buyer's due diligence process will often concentrate on the risks and rewards your financials present, especially your accounting documents such as cash flow statements, income statements, balance sheets, accounts receivable and accounts payable. They'll also be keen to scrutinise your growth plans and potential threats from competitors. Finally, they will want to be reassured about your company's stability in terms of your sales conversion rates, year-on-year growth patterns, and EBITDA records.

Things to think about

Selling your business to a financial buyer hinges on your history of financial stability and whether or not you've maintained an exceptionally low risk-reward ratio; you'll probably need an adjusted net profit of over a million pounds a year. Then, if you manage to achieve this and gain a sale, you can expect them to hold nothing back as they take over the business. They'll probably go in all guns blazing with a strong drive to maximise their profits within the shortest time possible. If it works out, your business will explode in size and profits, and even expand into new markets in the future.

As you've probably guessed, don't expect a financial buyer to be sentimental about your employees. Do, however, allow for the fact that they realise the importance of good people to any business. It's not uncommon for them to give incentives to important members of your senior leadership team, not only to reward them for good work but also to retain them in the future. In the accountancy take-over I mentioned above, the new owner has created an incentive plan for four members of the senior team of up to a million pounds each if they hit certain growth targets over the next three years.

The family office

This type of buyer is similar to the financial buyer in that it's a registered entity which serves as an investment holding company. Where it differs is that it's owned and managed either by professionals or by experienced members of a wealthy family who handle the family's investment portfolio. The people you typically find in a family office are affluent, business-minded individuals who not only want to safeguard but also grow the family's financial assets – for both current and future generations.

Another difference between the financial buyer and the family office is that the family office may well take a longer-term view of their investments. The financial buyer often looks to sell on an acquisition in three to four years so that they can pay back their investors. A family office, however, tends to use their own money for some or all of the transaction and is therefore more inclined to retain an acquisition with the view of swelling the family coffers using long-term dividend generation.

Many years ago, I helped to sell a business to a Scottish-based family office. The family had originally made its money through shipping but is now best known for publishing various regional newspapers and comics, such as *The Beano* and *The Dandy*. Over the years, the family office has invested in lots of other businesses in all kinds of sectors. Its aim is to keep the family's wealth intact for generations to come.

Their motivations

Family offices tend to be on the lookout for highly profitable companies that offer attractive, long-term returns. They're not interested in involving themselves in the day-to-day operations of the businesses they buy, but in reaping the financial rewards of their investments with minimal interference.

Their requirements

The high-net-worth individuals who run family offices have been around long enough to tell the difference between a struggling business and a stable one. They're not only interested in a robust balance sheet, they also want to establish your company's income potential over the long-term. Their aim is to buy a business that requires minimal supervision and is independent enough to remain profitable long after you've sold it to them, so that their fortune benefits their children and grandchildren over the decades.

Things to think about

Given the lack of involvement a family office expects to have in your business, they need to be confident that it can look after itself. To convince them of that, you have to show how well it's adapted to change over the years, and that your senior team is more than capable of running it well.

It's also worth knowing that, in comparison with financial buyers, there aren't many family offices in existence, so opportunities to be bought by one are few and far between. It's not every day you come across a family office that's in the market for a business like yours, even if they're sometimes prepared to pay a good price for a new acquisition.

The internal buyer

Your ideal buyer doesn't have to be a third party, but could be one or more of your own employees. There are two main ways for them to acquire your business:

- A management buyout (MBO)
- An employee ownership trust (EOT)

With an MBO, your management team buys you out either partially or wholly and runs the company themselves. With an EOT, your business is typically independently valued, and approval for the valuation is then often sought from HMRC before the shares are sold to a trust. Your employees become the beneficiaries of that trust – a bit like the John Lewis Partnership. This is an increasingly common way of exiting a business, often as a secondary option for owners who haven't been able to sell in other ways.

The advantages of selling to your employees

In an MBO or an EOT, the process often enables a smoother transition of ownership than if you were to sell to an outsider. Your management team and employees know your operations, internal culture and customers, and they have the technical skills and know-how to keep your company going. Who better to minimise disruption during the handover than them? What's more, if your people are financially invested in your business, they have every incentive to grow it and keep it profitable in the future.

From your point of view, selling to internal buyers also gives you the comfort of knowing that your hard work in building your brand and company traditions won't be undone by a financial or strategic buyer. You might even maintain a stake in your company so that you can share in its future success. What's more, an internal sale allows you to bypass some of the due diligence you have to go through with an external buyer, and to avoid disclosing sensitive information to a third party. This in turn can reduce the risk of disruption or a loss of competitive advantage during the sale process.

For an EOT, there are additional benefits to a traditional, broker-led, third-party sale. Most EOTs work best when the business has significant cash in the bank and a strong record of significant profit generation. If this is the case for you, you can reduce the risks associated with long-term, deferred payments by taking out a large initial lump sum, and because you don't need a broker, your transaction costs are lower. However, it's in the tax savings that you can win the most. The current tax-free aspects of an EOT mean that you're potentially able to sell for less than you would to other types of buyers, and still end up financially better off. For your employees in an EOT, they'll hopefully become super-engaged 'beneficiaries' of the company, which in turn allows them to earn up to a certain amount per year as a tax-free bonus.

Jonathan, one of my clients who owned a van rental business, put his company up for sale to external buyers with the expectation that he'd make £8 million. He received a good offer, but the buyer's plans for the business didn't sit comfortably with him, so he decided to withdraw from the process and go down the EOT route. The independent valuation resulted in him receiving just over £6.5 million, which at first appeared to be a worse deal financially, but not when tax was taken into account. Because Jonathan had nearly £2 million of cash in the company, and because the business generated profits of over £1 million a year, he was able to take out £3 million as an initial instalment – just under half the total value. Under the rules of an EOT, this was completely tax free.

The disadvantages of selling to your employees

The financial downside of selling to your employees is that, because staff often don't have the deep pockets that other types of buyers can have, you potentially won't receive the same level of initial consideration. You may well have to be prepared to wait for additional instalments, maybe over several years. For Jonathan, in my example above, this was a pill he was prepared to swallow. Not only did he have the comfort of leaving his firm in safe hands and the ease of making a smooth transition, but he was also paid £3 million immediately tax free. This was more than enough to keep him going until the rest of the funds came in.

Looking ahead to when you have a range of buyers showing an interest in your business, you'll probably find that they vary a lot in terms of size, motivation, experience with acquiring companies and spending power. That's why you need to know how to align your business to the five different types of buyer, which is what we explore in the next chapter.

SUMMARY POINTS

- Your aim is to get as many potential buyers as possible interested in your business, so as to create competition and maximise the sale value.
- Buyers come in different shapes and sizes, so be open-minded and don't limit yourself to one type.
- The five types of buyers are: individual, strategic, financial, family office and internal.
- Each of these types has its own motivations and requirements, which gives you different things to think about when deciding if you're going to sell to them.

ACTION POINTS

- Make a prioritised list of what's most important to you in a buyer, in terms of:
  - The depth of their pockets
  - Their plans for your employees
  - Their intention to continue with your brand and company culture
  - Their ability to effect a quick and smooth purchase and transition
- When you have your prioritised list, cross out the bottom two criteria; this leaves you with the two most important things that you're looking for in an acquirer.

4

What Does Your Buyer Want? Stepping Into Their Shoes

N ow that you know the difference between the five types of buyer, it's time to look at things from *their* point of view. What's important to them? What might attract them to buy your business? And how can you best communicate that acquiring your company is the most obvious solution to their needs? Remember that it's through having multiple, enthusiastic potential acquirers that you maximise your sale price, so you need to see things from more than one perspective.

We'll be covering these perspectives in detail later in this chapter, but first let's look at the common reasons why a company would want to acquire your business. In reality, the reasons vary wildly and may well prove difficult to decipher. However, if you can gain some insight into a buyer's motivations, you'll invariably be in the best place to maximise the value of your business throughout the sale process.

Common buyer motivations

Let's look at some of the most common buyer motivations that I've come across.

To increase their chances of success

While the barriers to entry in today's competitive business landscape are lower than ever, the costs of competing successfully continues to rise. Consequently, buying an established business, as opposed to launching one onto the market, is something that some buyers find less risky and hence more attractive, compared with the cost of establishing a leading business themselves.

To increase their market share

Buying another business that already has a strong foothold in the buyer's own market allows that buyer to increase their market share quickly. With this comes the ability to charge higher prices and negotiate larger economies of scale with suppliers, adding up to more profits and increased resilience in the marketplace.

A common example of businesses that do this are the private equity firms you met in the previous chapter. Some have acquisition strategies based on buying a number of companies that operate in similar markets, and then rolling them up into one large entity with a view to using the scale to sell at a higher multiple than they could with several smaller ones. But it's not only financial buyers who do this – it's also fairly common for an individual firm to buy another business to give itself more scale, purely in order to sell at a higher price in a few years' time. In fact, in the UK, many of the brokers that we regularly work with estimate that around 40% of businesses sold in any given year have themselves made an acquisition in the previous two years, for exactly this reason.

To gain access to new markets

Another way for a business to scale up is to take its products or services into new markets by buying a company that already operates there. If the acquirer is located in a particular area of the country, for instance, they might buy a business that sells similar products in a neighbouring region. Or they could acquire a firm that sells into a market that complements their original one. A client we worked with for a long time was a manufacturer of outdoor furniture for the hospitality industry. Buying a business that sold outdoor seating to racecourses and other leisure establishments enabled them to expand into that adjacent category.

Another example is a current client who operates in the medical devices sector. Their only significant customer is the NHS, and to sell to them they've had to go through the laborious process of becoming part of a framework agreement for a particular department or range of products. Selling their existing products into other framework areas or departments would mean trying to get accredited in those frameworks, so a quicker alternative is to buy a business that already has the agreements in place. This opens the door not only to selling the acquired company's products, but also being able to use the framework for their own.

To gain access to new people and expertise

This is particularly common with large companies that buy small ones. The big business gains the dynamism that made the start-up a success, which helps them to become more dynamic themselves, or they acquire access to bespoke technology that only the smaller business can provide.

While all buyers aim to grow or protect their assets, it's also important to remember that no matter what their goals are, they want to see that you've worked on delivering the ten drivers of business value that we explored in Chapter 2. They look for strong financial performance over the last few years, and a credible scale-up plan that you've developed in detail. They want to be assured that the revenue from your business will be secure, whether it be through subscriptions or a pipeline of new work. They seek a company with a standout brand and clearly defined USPs that its customers value, a company that has a strong management team and a diverse and loyal customer base, and that isn't overly reliant on you as the owner. And they also need to be assured that you have enough working capital so they will not have to fund your day-to-day operations out of their own pockets, and that you've protected your intellectual property.

The five types of buyer

Now that we've summarised some of the common motivations for buyers, let's look at the five types of buyer and their specific aims:

1. The individual buyer
2. The strategic buyer
3. The financial buyer
4. The family office
5. The internal buyer

It's well worth investing time in understanding what each of these focus on when they look to buy a business, because it will help you to position your company in the right way for them. To help you put yourself in their shoes in each case, I've presented the first bit of information as if they were writing it themselves.

The individual buyer

What they're thinking

'I'm looking for a small business that will deliver me a solid, recurring income. I'd prefer it to be in a sector I know well or am interested in, but that's not essential; my main aim is to give myself financial freedom and have control over my own destiny. My biggest concern about the process is that I've never bought a business before, so I'm not completely sure what I'm doing. I'm also anxious about finding skeletons in the cupboard later, as I know from experience what a nightmare the wrong people or poorly managed finances can be. This is my money I'm spending and it's my business that I'll be owning, so it's personal – I can't afford to make a mistake.'

What the individual buyer needs from you

With an individual buyer who's potentially inexperienced, one of the main things to bear in mind is that they're unsure what all the sales terminology means, what the steps in the buying process are, and how they can best decide whether your company is a good fit for them. These factors play a part in how you should deal with them. It's important to explain, in a step-by-step way, why you'd be a good acquisition. You may sometimes have to go further with this than with other types of acquirer because the individual buyer doesn't always know the right questions to ask. So lead them carefully and transparently through how you've set up your business, the way it works, how it will continue to run well without you, and why all this means that it's a great investment for them. Don't assume that any of it is obvious. At the same time, avoid overwhelming them with detail; apart from their accountant, they probably won't have a lot of help with the due diligence process, so they need you to make things as simple as possible (while still being open and honest).

The strategic buyer

What they're thinking

'I'm looking for an acquisition that will complement my existing business, not only in terms of what the company does but also in its financial and operational synergies with my own. It needs to help me grow my market share, reduce my costs, expand into new products and markets, or give me a lever to build my bottom line in some other way. I've bought businesses before, so I know what I'm doing, but I still need to be sure that my next acquisition is the right one. I won't buy anything that doesn't pass the due diligence test.'

What the strategic buyer needs from you

To sell to a strategic buyer, you need to think like one. What can your company offer in terms of strategic fit to a business like theirs? This comes down to you knowing your strengths *from their point of view*. Do you have access to specific markets that would be difficult for them to reach without a business such as yours? A contracted-in set of regular customers versus their own ad hoc client base? Unique skills or technology that could complement theirs? A strong reputation for a certain type of product that complements theirs? Mentally step outside your business so that you can see it from these angles.

How you describe the value inherent in your business to a strategic buyer is also important – they need to see without a doubt that they can't replicate what you offer without vast expense or risk. If you don't map out a clear path to profits for them, they may just view your business as giving them more of the same. A strategic buyer doesn't necessarily have the skills to scale a business quickly, so they may need you to join the dots when it comes to showing them how to make use of your strengths. This is the kind of information that will enable them to justify paying a premium for your company.

It's also important to back up the opportunity with credible evidence. For this, data is key, as it is data that will support your story of future growth the buyer is looking for. And while we're on the subject of data, if you're selling to a competitor, there are clearly risks associated with giving away too much information throughout the sale process. You need to strike a balance between openness and maintaining confidentiality, for instance by numbering rather than naming your clients.

The financial buyer

What they're thinking

'I'm looking for a business that I can grow, scale and sell within the next few years. It's all about return on investment for me, because I'll be using the profit from the sale to pay back my investors and deliver a great return for them and ourselves. So the key things I'll be taking into account are a company's working capital position, level of profitability, and growth potential, and I'm prepared to pay for it if I think it's the right opportunity. It might be that I can integrate the business with others in my portfolio, giving me economies of scale and the ability to build a single, larger entity that I could sell on for a larger multiple. Given that I'm not planning on running the business myself, I also want a management team with the right skills and experience. My due diligence team will make sure that all the details are forensically researched.'

What the financial buyer needs from you

Just like any other acquirer, a financial buyer wants to buy a company that satisfies the ten drivers of business value that we talked about earlier, but foremost in their mind is whether they can rapidly scale your business before selling it on. Alongside that, they need to be confident that you have a management team capable of delivering the growth they need. That's why your growth plan needs to be watertight, and your management team as adept at talking about it as you are.

A financial buyer will also crawl through your data in detail, including your accounts and anything that may indicate an over-reliance on key customers, suppliers and members of staff. They want to know where your business market is heading and what risk factors are associated with it, including any potential economic and legislative changes. That's why you need to have all the facts and figures to hand and be prepared for them to be scrutinised – your financial ratios, including your EBITDA, and your working capital level are key. It's often a highly impersonal process for a financial buyer: are they better off investing their money into buying your company, or another one? Or would they get more bang for their buck by buying another asset altogether? Your job is to convince them that your business has the solid financial base and the potential for rapid scale that they're looking for.

The family office

What they're thinking

'I want to buy a business that will deliver a great return on our investment for years to come. It's my responsibility to ensure the long-term health of the family assets, so a company that's been well run, that can continue working without the owner, and that is a safe bet to grow its revenue and profits in the future, is our ideal acquisition. I've done this many times before so I know what I'm looking for: a company that I can rely on to enhance our family's wealth-creation activities.'

What the family office needs from you

Their requirements are similar to those of the financial buyer, with the exception that they want to be assured of the long-term viability of your business. You need to be just as prepared for the rigour and depth of their due diligence, but rather than positioning your company as one that's ripe for scaling and selling over the next few years, you should outline how it can deliver reliable profits for the next decade or two.

The internal buyer

What they're thinking

For your senior team in a management buyout (MBO): 'It's exciting to think that we could own and run our company ourselves. While it's a big step to take, I can see a time in the future when we'll have paid off our debt to the current owner or founder and can take some nice dividends for ourselves. Then, when I want to leave, I can sell my share to someone else and reap the rewards of my investment. My only worry is how we're going to raise the cash. We'll need to put in some money of our own, then the rest of our initial payment will probably have to come from either the bank or a private equity house. We'll need to negotiate with the business owner to pay off the rest over the next few years. It's a bit daunting, especially given that we'll have to generate enough profits for the instalments.'

For your employees in an employee ownership trust (EOT): 'I'll carry on doing the same job as normal, but along with my existing colleagues, we'll all finally have a sense that we really have a stake in our future success. What's more, we'll have the chance to earn a tax-free bonus each year, and it will be rewarding to be a beneficiary of a company that I've been working in for a while. What's not to like?'

What the internal buyer needs from you

When you sell to your management team or hand over your business to all of your employees via a trust board, you're leading them on a first-time journey. Due diligence isn't the main thing that they're concerned about and they're probably intimate with the company's inner workings already, or at the very least your management team is. What they do need, however, is clear and honest guidance from you about how the process works and what their responsibilities are.

In an MBO, your team's top issue is raising enough money to pay you an initial sum and later instalments, probably over a number of years. You may need to help them with this, for instance by giving your backing to any finance deal they secure or being willing to wait longer for your money than you might ideally like. Your sale and purchase agreement with them should contain provisions and securities for what happens if they fail to pay you on time.

In an EOT, your employees don't have to raise the money themselves to buy you out, but the trust may well do if you require an initial consideration that can't be met entirely from cash reserves. The trust board will often have a professional trustee to oversee the trust's obligations, and to ensure that the new management team runs the company properly and in a manner that ensures you're paid in line with the sale agreement. Staged payments are most likely to have to be funded from the business' future profits, and hence the governance of the management team and its obligations to you are critical. As with an MBO, you may well have to wait longer for your money than if you were to sell to an external buyer.

Whatever buyer types you aim at, pitching your

business in the right way involves you standing well back and seeing the transaction through their eyes. Not only that, but you need to recognise that, even within each of the five types, there's a variation in individual needs, motivations and goals, and in people's understanding of the process. This is really hard to do, because you're intimately familiar with your company and not used to looking at it through the lens of a purchaser. It's a bit like when you go home each evening – the stain on the ceiling that's been there for years is invisible to you, as is the beautiful fireplace that made you think, 'I've got to live here.' That's why working with an experienced business sale advisor can be helpful because they won't have the emotional attachment to your business that comes from years of nurturing it but can see it objectively.

Now that we've explored the different buyer types, we'll move on to the next big question: how long will it take to sell your business?

SUMMARY POINTS

- All buyers have one thing in common: they want to grow or protect their assets and see acquiring a business as the best way of doing that.
- Each of the five types of buyer has their own assumptions, concerns, aims and levels of knowledge about the process.
- If you can speak to a buyer in their language, you stand a higher chance of attracting multiple offers and boosting your sale price.

- To do that, you need to understand how they think about buying a business like yours.

ACTION POINTS

- In the last chapter, you identified the two most important things you're looking for in a buyer. Now that you've read this one, has anything changed?
- Make a list of factors that would attract acquirers to your company and those that would give them pause for thought.
- How can you describe your business' positive features in ways that speak to the different buyer types?

5

How Long Will It Take?
The Timeline To Sale

The first question I'm asked by every entrepreneur when we first meet is, 'If I work with you, how long will it take to sell my business?' No matter what the answer, it's invariably longer than they think.

Selling your business is a journey, and like all journeys, it takes time. From making the monumental decision to put your company on the market, to the day when that all-important sum of money appears in your bank account, there are many steps along the way. We've already discussed the importance of dedicating time to ensuring that the ten drivers of business value are optimised in your business. It's not unusual for the whole process of establishing the drivers, appointing your deal team, marketing the business for sale, and ultimately completing the sale, to take two to three years.

That said, in the last year, I had a client who received an unsolicited approach to sell their residential lettings business, and the whole process took less than four months from the initial approach to completing the deal. For the seller, the approach came at exactly the right time, as he and his family were already thinking about emigrating and the offer was more than the valuation they'd previously received from an independent valuer. Sometimes, I guess the stars just align!

This chapter is, nonetheless, devoted to all things timing related. I'll start by outlining how you know when it's the right time to sell, and then move on to a timeline of the entire sale process.

When to sell your business

Choosing the right moment to put your company on the market is an important one, because it's one of the deciding factors in whether you gain the best possible price for it. So how do you know when that moment is? There's no one-size-fits-all answer, but there are three main things to take into account:

1. The condition of your market
2. Your business performance
3. Your personal goals and readiness

The condition of your market

Macro-economic factors such as GDP growth, unemployment rates, consumer spending trends and interest rates determine whether or not you'll be sowing your seeds in fertile ground if you put your company up for sale. The demand to buy businesses tends to go up in times of strong economic growth because acquirers have money to spend, but there are exceptions to this rule. If your company is a strong performer and likely to do even better in the future, there will often be someone who wants to buy it no matter what the environment.

Narrowing our focus, how your particular sector is performing also needs considering, because individual industries don't always follow the national trend. During the Covid pandemic, for instance, I wouldn't have wanted to be selling a hospitality business, but web-conferencing services rocketed in value. Our reliance on home-based IT has now led to huge buyer demand for IT support companies with strong recurring incomes.

Competition within your sector is also critical. Who are your industry disruptors? How are technologies such as AI, cryptocurrencies and automation going to change the way that work is done? What regulatory shifts are on the horizon? On top of that, local supply and demand dynamics, such as population growth, demographic trends, and regional economic activity, can play a part in when you should sell. If you have a locally based business, how strong is your market right now? Would a buyer be attracted to invest in it? And what does all this mean for when you should sell your business?

Knowing your market conditions goes further than

just deciding when to sell, important though that is. It also makes a difference when it comes to creating your marketing materials for sale. When you put thought into the strengths and weaknesses of your business relative to what's going on in the wider economy, your industry and your local area, you create a convincing story about why your business is a great purchase for someone else.

Your business performance

Here we return to the ten drivers of business value. Buyers are keen to get their hands on companies that have a strong track record of profitability, a healthy cash flow and sustainable growth potential. The latter is key. I often see owners putting their businesses up for sale when their revenues and profits are already maxed out, only to struggle to generate interest because (with the possible exception of individual buyers) acquirers want an investment that's guaranteed to grow.

That means you need to evaluate your company's historical growth rates. Sustainable and profitable growth signals to buyers that there's a demand for what you do, and it goes without saying that a business with strong margins will receive a higher valuation than one that doesn't. Also important is where your revenue comes from, as the degree to which your customers are locked in is an indication of how likely a new owner will be to retain them. So, if you have an increasing and recurring income, it might be the right time to sell. If not, you have work to do.

Think about your competitive positioning as well. As business owners, we're often rather generous to ourselves on this front and can have an inflated view of how well we're doing in the marketplace. I sometimes meet company owners who are convinced that it's the right time to sell because they've grown by 10% over the past two years. 'That's great,' I say, 'but would you feel as good if I told you that your competitors have grown by 20%?' The truth is that they don't actually know how well their competitors are doing – something that will quickly be revealed by an acquirer's due diligence. Ask yourself, where are you placed in your market compared to others? What's your market share? And is your brand recognised and distinctive?

Speaking of due diligence, how in-shape are your financial records? This can partly determine when you sell, because there's nothing that will put off a prospective buyer more than overly complicated or opaque financial reports. If they're not able to navigate your records easily, they won't want to buy your business. It might be that you need time to put your house in order, not only with your record-keeping but also your contracts with suppliers, employees and contractors.

The good thing about these internal business factors is that they're largely under your control. You can decide how much you want to improve them and how much you don't, and this will dictate whether you sell quickly for less or slowly for more. It really is up to you.

Your personal goals and readiness

Selling your business is a deeply personal decision, and whether you get it right or wrong can have a profound impact on the rest of your life. It might be that you want to retire, have free time to do fun and interesting things, or maybe start another business. Whatever your aspirations, it's important to know what kind of lifestyle you dream of and, just as importantly, how much money you'll need to fund it off the back of your company's sale.

We cover how to value your business in the following chapter, but it's relevant here because your company's current worth can affect when you decide to sell. You might have mortgaged your house or taken out personal loans to support your business. If so, what kind of sale figure do you need to pay off your debts and then live the life you want? If your business' value is effectively your pension, what's the minimum price that allows you to have financial security for you and your family? Remember to factor tax obligations into this.

Part of financial planning is thinking about your legacy. This could be monetary, if you want to give funds to those who are important to you, either in this life or the next. Alternatively, it might mean a lot to you to sell your company to an acquirer who will preserve your brand, culture and people – someone who shares your vision and values. This can have an influence on when you sell, because you may want to wait for the right buyer before you hand over your precious business.

One of my clients who sold his company wasn't too worried about his personal legacy, but was concerned about his daughter, who had learning difficulties and had worked for him for many years. She did a great job, but he worried that a new owner might not see it that way. In the end, we found a buyer who was keen to keep her on and was understanding about her challenges, which was hugely reassuring for him.

Another emotional element of deciding when to sell is how much appetite you have to carry on with your business. I've worked with many clients who want to sell up simply because they've run out of enthusiasm or energy for the continuous battle that's associated with running a company. There's no doubt that they could, if they wanted, grow their business even further and more profitably, then sell it for much more than if they took it to market now. But they don't want to, and as their coach and advisor, I have to respect that they know when the time is right. My job is to help them secure the maximum value from their business whenever they decide to sell.

Finally, think about how prepared you are to let go of your business and embrace a new chapter in your life. 'It's been my whole life', is a phrase I often hear from prospective sellers when they talk about running their companies. Are you really ready to surrender the reins? Selling up can stir up a lot of feelings – pride, nostalgia, uncertainty about the future – so you may want some time to come to terms with the huge change that you're about to go through.

The timeline to sale

There's no concrete timeline for selling a business as each situation is different, but it's important that you have a realistic idea about the minimum and maximum amounts of time that it could take. You might be surprised at the length of some of the phases, but there's nothing to say that you can't progress your sale more quickly if you work hard and already have the key pillars in place. It's also possible to carry out some tasks concurrently rather than sequentially.

In terms of what the steps in the process are, I'll go through them in a lot more detail in the second half of the book. The timeline below is just to give you an overview of the selling journey; think of it as a roadmap that takes you from making the decision to sell all the way through to tying up the loose ends.

There are five phases:

1. Preparation (three to twelve months before listing)
2. Marketing and listing (three to six months)
3. Negotiation and due diligence (three to six months)
4. Purchase agreement and closing (one to three months)
5. Transition and post-sale integration (one to six months after closing)

Phase 1: preparation (three to twelve months before listing)

If your business is sale-ready and performing strongly on all ten drivers of business value, you'll probably whistle through this phase in nearer three months than twelve. If not, you have to decide how much you want to delay the sale in order to get a better price. There's also work to be done to put your paperwork in order, as this can scupper the sale during the due diligence process if you're not careful. Trust me when I say that you really don't want to be doing this after you receive an offer.

There are three elements to this phase:

- Assessment and preparation
- Business valuation
- Putting together your deal team

Assessment and preparation

- Assess how your company is performing according to the ten drivers of business value. Work out what needs improvement, develop a plan, and put it into action.
- Prepare the financial paperwork, including income statements, balance sheets and cash flow statements. Ensure that your financial records are accurate and up to date.
- Organise your operational records, including employee contracts, leases and customer

agreements. Review your key supplier contracts to identify any liabilities or risks that may concern an acquirer. For instance, is there anything in your IT supplier's contract that prevents them from pulling the plug and leaving you without any support?

- Carry out a comprehensive review of your legal documentation, including corporate records, intellectual property rights and regulatory compliance. There's probably more to do here than you think. I often find that business owners don't have proper shareholder agreements for all their shareholders, or don't have intellectual property rights correctly filed. This needs to be addressed now.

Business valuation

- Few businesses have had a formal valuation of their company done, but doing this is important because it tells you what's realistic. You don't want to spend an inordinate amount of time and effort taking your business to market only to discover that it was never going to give you what you needed to live the life you want. So, work with valuation professionals to determine a fair range of selling prices, taking into account tax implications as well. This can take three months or more, depending on how large or complex your business is and whether you need a formally approved valuation by HMRC in the case of an employee ownership trust.

Putting together your deal team

- Assemble a qualified deal team to help you through the sale process. I detail who the members of this team should be in Chapter 7.

Phase 2: marketing and listing (three to six months)

Much of the work around marketing and listing your business for sale will be carried out by your chosen broker or corporate finance partner (detailed in Chapter 8), but it's important that you know what happens so you can plan for the time it will take. There are two activities in this phase:

1. **Developing marketing materials:** Your broker creates marketing materials, including the information memorandum, executive summary and 'teaser' document.

2. **Identifying potential buyers:** Your broker creates a list of potential acquirers, working with you to refine it. They then send your teaser document to the list, and secure nondisclosure agreements with interested parties.

Phase 3: negotiation and due diligence (three to six months)

As with the marketing and listing phase, this is largely carried out by your broker and is detailed in Chapters 8, 9 and 10. Where you come in is during the face-to-face discussions with prospective buyers, and the due diligence process. You'll be extremely glad that you did the preparation work in Phase 1 at this point.

There are two activities in this phase:

1. **Engaging with interested buyers (one to three months after listing):**

   - Your broker follows up with the people to whom they've sent the teaser document and sends them the information memorandum.

   - You and your broker narrow down the offers you receive.

   - This is followed by a series of discussions and meetings between you, your potential buyers and your broker.

   - You select your preferred buyer, and they produce a heads of terms, or letter of intent, that summarises the deal. (I'll refer to this only as the heads of terms from now on.)

2. **Due Diligence Process (two to four months after listing):**

   - Your buyer creates their shopping list of the documents that they want to see as part of their due diligence.

– To facilitate this, you upload your documents to a data room, which is a secure depository for all your information.

If you want to be prepared ahead of time with the information you'll need to provide for due diligence, I've created a helpful checklist. Please use it to give yourself a heads-up. It's at: www.chalkhillblue.org /ddchecklist.

Phase 4: purchase agreement and closing (one to three months)

Assuming that Phase 3 has gone well, the lawyers on both sides are now able to get to work on the sale and purchase agreement as detailed in Chapter 11. There are two sets of activities in this phase:

1. **Negotiating the purchase agreement (one to two months before closing):**
   – Your lawyers get their teeth into the legal nitty gritty by negotiating with your buyer's lawyers about the terms in the purchase agreement.
   – Both parties sign the final agreement, and the deal is sealed.

2. **The closing process (two to three months after signing the purchase agreement):**
   – You and your deal team co-ordinate the closing process to finalise the transaction and transfer your business assets.

- You sign closing documents to effect the transfer of ownership.
- You work with your acquirer to finalise your company's completion accounts, pay off necessary business debts, and ensure that the agreed amount of working capital is left in the business.
- Your buyer disburses funds to shareholders, creditors and other stakeholders.

Phase 5: transition and post-sale integration (one to twelve months after closing)

What comes next is a period of transition of anywhere between one and six months – sometimes longer. This depends on the complexity of the deal and whether it's an asset- or share-based sale. Then there are the obvious parts of handing over, such as bringing the new owner up to speed on how things work in your business. You might also be required to stay on for a while to help with the transition.

There are two elements to this phase:

1. **Transition planning (one to three months after closing):**
   - Develop a transition plan to facilitate a smooth handover to the new owner.
   - Give training and support to the new owner to make the transition as smooth as possible.
   - Address post-sale commitments or warranties outlined in the purchase agreement.

2. **Post-sale integration (three to twelve months after closing):**

   - Work with the new owner to support the post-sale integration.

   - Monitor key performance indicators, financial metrics and operational benchmarks to assess the business' performance post-sale – making any changes necessary to help the owner maximise the value of their purchase.

   - Maintain communication with the new owner and stakeholders to address any problems.

If, when looking at this entire timeline, you think that it seems pretty onerous, you'd be right. It's a huge task to sell a company – one that most owners find all-consuming. And I hate to say it, but there's more. During this entire process, from deciding to sell to sealing the deal, you will also have to focus on running and growing your business. It's easy to become distracted from your operations when your head is buried in marketing and legal documents, but you can't let that happen. Imagine that your business is valued at £5 million, and your net profits drop by £250,000 in the year running up to the sale. At a four times multiple, that's £1 million off the purchase price. This is why having a hands-on management team that takes care of the day-to-day running of your company is so important, as it makes it easier for you to absorb yourself in the sale without there being a knock-on effect on your business performance.

In the next chapter, we'll cover the bit you've been waiting for: working out how much your company is worth.

SUMMARY POINTS

- The right time to sell your business depends on the condition of your market, your business performance, and your personal goals and readiness.
- Selling a company can take two to three years, so you have to be prepared for the long haul.
- There are five phases in the timeline to sale: preparation, marketing and listing, negotiation and due diligence, the purchase agreement and closing, and finally the transition and post-sale integration.
- During all of this, it's important to keep growing your business profitably.

ACTION POINTS

- Think about the three factors involved in deciding when you sell your business. For each one, decide the key areas that are most relevant to you.
- From that, estimate when you think you'll be ready to put your company up for sale.

- Something that you can get started on straightaway is putting your paperwork in order. Carry out a review of all your documentation, both legal and financial, and identify where there are gaps to fill. You can find a list at www.chalkhillblue.org/ddchecklist.

6

What's It Worth? How To Value Your Company

How much is your company worth? This is the million-dollar question, and one to which there's both a short and a long answer. The short answer is that your company is worth the maximum somebody is prepared to pay for it. The long answer is what I'll spend the rest of this chapter exploring, as we decipher the options you have for calculating a realistic number. By the end, you'll understand why valuations vary so much, the different ways of valuing a business, how your prospective buyers will consider your valuation, and who can help you through this complicated process.

It's important to get your valuation right because it's a critical part of your exit planning process. Our own surveys, and those of many brokers, suggest that 58% of business owners have never had their businesses formally valued. The problem this gives them is that they don't have a reliable value range to help them decide whether they want to sell now, later, or maybe not at all. This is the part of the book in which I'm going to get most granular and forensic, so apologies in advance for all the detail, but it's worth understanding the nuances so that you can make the best decision for you.

Why valuations vary

One of the frustrating things about pinning a value on your business is that, depending on who you ask and when, you'll receive a different answer. It's like trying to catch an eel that keeps slithering through your fingers. For that reason, any decent valuation will give you a range of figures and may well discuss how different types of buyers use different valuation methodologies. In a moment, you'll learn why some ways of valuing a business are more relevant to your situation than others, but for now, let's look at what factors can influence your valuation figure.

Market conditions

Imagine two identical businesses, each brought to market during different economic cycles. Will they sell for the same sum? Probably not. That's because market conditions play a significant role in shaping buyers' perceptions of your company's value. When economic times are good, they may feel optimistic about growing your business and be inclined to pay more for it. Conversely, the opposite is true during down times, when they see it as a riskier venture. The same is true for ups and downs in the market affecting your particular industry.

Subjectivity

Facts such as your market size, profit margins and historical sales figures are indisputable. What varies are the interpretations that people place on them. Different buyers apply different methodologies, make differing assumptions and emphasise different data points. It's *humans* who create valuations, not machines, and everyone has their own goals, experiences and biases. For instance, a strategic buyer might value the fact that a business is successful in a market they're keen to enter and therefore be prepared to pay over the odds for it, whereas a financial buyer would only be interested in the same business if they could see rapid growth potential.

Assumptions and projections

Given that an acquirer is buying the future of your business, your valuation inevitably depends on what projections they make about that future. Small changes in assumptions about revenue growth, profit margins, capital expenditure and working capital requirements can lead to large disparities in valuations.

Simon, a recent client of ours in the beauty equipment industry, ended up selling his company successfully, but it almost didn't happen. Before working with us, he'd valued his business using an unfounded and arguably unrealistic projection of its future growth. Not only had his business never achieved that kind of performance in its twenty-year history, but he also had no plan for how it could happen, other than a new owner managing it differently. Unsurprisingly, after Simon had taken his business to market, none of the interested buyers was prepared to value it on that basis, choosing instead an average of the last three years' performance and the income it generated for the owner.

Having failed to secure an acceptable offer for his business with his first attempt, we were able to highlight the obvious flaws in his initial approach and help Simon re-work his growth plans. This resulted in him securing a much-improved pipeline of future orders. We could then substantiate how a buyer could credibly expect to generate a decent return on their investment and re-present the business for sale through the same broker. In the end, Simon and his wife received an offer which was some 15% above his initial expectation.

Timing

A business evolves over time. There will always be changes in performance, market conditions, the competition and external regulations, and these have an impact on what it can sell for at any given moment.

Put your business up for sale when you're the strongest player in your market, and you're likely to be in a better position than when a well-funded competitor has just got in on the act.

Methodology

Different valuation methods emphasise different aspects of your financials and prospects, and can therefore have a significant impact on the figure you end up with. To see what I mean, let's have a look at the different valuation methods available.

Valuation methods

There are six main ways of valuing a business, each with its own strengths and weaknesses, and you need to understand the nuances of each method if you're to gain an accurate and meaningful estimate. Let's look at each of the six methods in turn:

1. Discounted cash flow (DCF)
2. Comparable company analysis (CCA)
3. Precedent transactions
4. EBITDA multiple
5. Adjusted EBITDA
6. Seller's discretionary earnings (SDE)

Discounted cash flow (DCF)

This is one of the most widely used valuation methods. In it, your future cash flows are estimated and then discounted using the cost of capital to give a present value. The method accounts for the 'time value' of money (money today is worth more than money tomorrow) and the risks associated with predicting the future.

Pros: It captures the intrinsic value of your business by considering its future financial health. You can also apply a sensitivity analysis, in which you explore different scenarios and assumptions.

Cons: DCF is highly sensitive to assumptions about future cash flows, discount rates and terminal values. A small change to one of these can lead to a large difference in valuation, so it's a method that's vulnerable to subjective judgements.

Comparable company analysis (CCA)

When people first come to me for help with selling their businesses, I find that this is the method they've most often used, mainly because it seems so logical. In it, you compare your company's financial metrics to those of a similar business that's recently sold, to create an estimated valuation. It relies on the principle of market efficiency, which says that similar companies should have similar valuations.

Pros: CCA is relatively straightforward, which means you can make quick comparisons between different companies to come up with a valuation.

Cons: How do you know what similar businesses have actually sold for? Figures are rarely published, let alone the intricacies of the terms and conditions that were part of the deal. You're limited to comparing your business with publicly listed companies in the same industry. What's more, differences between businesses in terms of models, growth prospects and other variances can distort your valuation. Also, for a comparison to be useful, it has to assume that the type of buyer is similar too.

Precedent transactions

This method involves analysing past mergers and acquisitions within your industry to come up with a valuation, and – unlike CCA – only tends to be used with larger transactions where the data is more readily available. It assumes that the value paid in previous transactions reflects the fair value of similar businesses.

Pros: Because it's based on real-world transaction data, it reflects market sentiment and actual deal prices.

Cons: Data on precedent transactions may not be easily available, or the deals may not be directly comparable to your business. There can be differences in deal structures, timings and market conditions which distort the picture.

EBITDA multiple

EBITDA represents a company's earnings before accounting for interest, tax, depreciation and amortisation, giving a measure of its operational profitability. The EBITDA multiple method involves applying a multiple to a company's EBITDA to come up with a figure that represents it's worth.

Pros: It's simple to calculate and widely used, particularly in sectors where capital expenditures and depreciation are significant elements of a company's value. It also focuses on a company's earnings before nonoperating expenses, thereby giving a value that's based on how well the business is run.

Cons: It may not fully account for differences in capital structure, tax rates, or growth prospects. In addition, it can be skewed by factors such as one-off expenses and changes in working capital.

Adjusted EBITDA

This is a more commonly used method than EBITDA multiple. It refines it by excluding one-off expenses, such as that extra pension contribution you made last year, or expenses related to acquisitions. Its aim is to give a clear picture of your company's operational performance and ability to generate cash.

Pros: It gives a more accurate picture of your company's core earnings than EBITDA multiple alone by eliminating nonrecurring and nonoperational expenses. As a result, it provides a clearer basis for comparison across companies and industries.

Cons: It can be subjective. I've often seen buyers and sellers disagreeing on key items such as the cost of staff to replace existing shareholders. Similarly, excessive adjustments or inconsistencies in the way that it's carried out can throw up questions about how reliable it is.

Seller's discretionary earnings (SDE)

This method is commonly used for small, owner-operated businesses. It represents the earnings available to the owner-operator, taking into account the owner's salary and the company's net income, depreciation, interest and discretionary expenses.

Pros: It gives an accurate reflection of a small business' true earning potential, and it's a simple approach for companies with limited financial resources and uncomplicated structures. For these reasons, it's often used by individual buyers.

Cons: SDE may not capture the full value of the business, particularly if the owner's compensation is above or below market rates. It may also overlook potential growth opportunities or risks that could affect future earnings. For this reason, valuations using SDE are often on the conservative side.

Looking at all of these valuation methods, you can see that each offers insights into what a company is worth but that no single one is perfect. When you're valuing your business, you need to take into account the nature of your business, the data you have available, and the dynamics of your industry. Often, the best answer is to use a combination of methods so that you can give yourself the most reliable range of figures.

Key terminology

As I went through the valuation methods, I touched on the fact that different types of buyers have differing perspectives on how best to value a business. In addition to that, there are at least ten valuation concepts which, depending on an acquirer's goals and preferences, can also affect how they come up with a valuation. It's important that you understand the terminology and the ideas behind these concepts as they'll almost certainly come up during the selling process.

Going concern. This is a phrase that you often hear accountants use. What they mean by it is that, if a business generates profits and is likely to continue doing so in the future, it's a 'going concern'. It's a way of evaluating its long-term viability and attractiveness as an investment.

Terminal value. This is about a business' long-term value beyond the forecasted period used by the seller. It considers factors such as perpetual growth rates, market multiples and exit strategies if the new owner were to sell the business in the future. Private equity buyers often use this term, which isn't surprising when you consider that their strategy is often to buy a company with a view to selling it in a few years' time.

Risk and return. This one is self-explanatory. What return will an acquirer be likely to receive if they buy your company? Is it better than putting the same amount of money in the bank or investing it in something else?

Synergy. This is particularly important to the strategic buyer. Will buying your business give them access to new markets where they can sell their existing products, or to new products for their existing markets? There may be other synergies that are possible, too. The extent to which they can be convinced of those synergies, and their future value, goes a long way towards determining the price they'll be prepared to pay for your company.

Liquidity. This is related to the concept of risk and return. Buyers evaluate the liquidity of your business because they want to know how much cash they might need to inject to keep it afloat. If sales were to drop one month, how long would it be before they had to put in their own money to cover expenses? And if they were to want to sell it again quickly and at a good price, would that be possible given the liquidity (or otherwise) of the assets?

Control premium. When someone buys a majority stake in a business, or acquires it outright, they often pay a premium for the benefit that it gives them. That's because being a majority shareholder allows them to make decisions without having to defer to others. As an example, my business partners and I once bought a 50% share in an IT support services business. That initially meant that we had no overall control of the company, but equally, we didn't pay a control premium for the privilege. A year further down the line, however, we were able to acquire some additional equity from another minority shareholder, which gave us a majority stake.

Illiquidity discount. If your business has assets that aren't liquid and so can't immediately be sold, this might reduce the amount a buyer is prepared to pay for it. For instance, if your business is committed to a five-year lease on its offices and a buyer wants to move your employees to its own building to save costs, the lease commitment would reduce your company's value in their eyes.

My partner and I recently bid for another small IT support firm, but the company was committed to a long-term lease that didn't have a break clause. Needless to say, our offer reflected that commitment and the reduced economies of scale that we were likely to achieve by not being able to relocate the business into our existing offices.

Enterprise value versus equity value. This is a technical one. Buyers distinguish between enterprise value and equity value to understand the capital structure implications of their investment. Enterprise value represents the total value of the business including debt and equity components, while equity value reflects the value attributed only to its shareholders. In small to mid-market transactions, the enterprise value is what you most often see used, but if your business is bought by a listed company, they may look at the deal from an equity value perspective.

Market sentiment. Understanding market sentiment helps buyers to predict market dynamics, and to gauge it, they analyse market trends and investor sentiment. It's a subjective process but that doesn't make it any less important. A buyer's perception is their reality, so if they think that your company's market is the next big thing, they'll be prepared to pay a premium.

Regulatory environment. Buyers analyse regulatory trends, changes in legislation and any compliance requirements that are relevant to your business. This is with the aim of predicting how much risk they'd be taking on if they were to buy it. For instance, if your firm sells wood burners and the government announces a new law to restrict their use, your future revenue projections are now in doubt. Any buyer who had already shown an interest would review their offer, but the conclusion they come to might depend on what kind of acquirer they are. A financial buyer would probably be put off by this change, but an individual buyer may maintain their interest if they thought they could still earn a good income from your business. This, by the way, is one of the reasons that it's important to market your company to a broad range of buyers.

I hope that you've found these valuation concepts from a buyer's perspective useful. When you know what acquirers are thinking when they look at your business, and how they make decisions aligned with their investment objectives and attitude to risk, you can discuss the terms of the sale from an educated viewpoint.

Help with valuing your business

As you'll have seen by now, valuing a business is no small undertaking. It's complicated, subjective and technical. Luckily, there are professionals who can help you to pick your way through the valuation minefield, each of them bringing their own type of expertise. They are:

- Brokers
- Mergers & Acquisitions (M&A) firms
- Accountants
- Specialist valuers

Brokers. These specialise in facilitating the sale and purchase of a business. While their primary role is to match you with buyers, many also offer business valuation services. Brokers help you to calculate an asking price for your company by using their knowledge of market conditions, industry trends and transactional data. A note of caution: brokers have a vested interest in erring on the higher end of the valuation so as to encourage you to choose them. Just be aware that some are less scrupulous than others on that front.

Mergers & Acquisitions (M&A) firms. These advise companies on mergers, acquisitions and divestitures, and have teams of analysts and advisors dedicated to business valuation. To do this, they use sophisticated valuation techniques while also looking at a company's value from a strategic angle, incorporating factors such as synergies, market positioning and the competitive landscape. They tend to be most useful for large-scale or complex business sales.

Accountants. Certified public accountants and accounting firms play a crucial role in business valuation, particularly in the context of financial reporting, taxation and litigation support. They use their expertise to conduct valuations for a variety of purposes, including financial reporting and tax planning. Because accountants' valuations adhere to rigorous accounting standards and regulatory requirements, they give assurance and credibility to stakeholders.

Specialist valuers. Although specialist valuers usually provide independent valuations across a wide range of industries and asset classes, they often have expertise in specific industries or types of assets. Specialist valuers may focus on areas such as intellectual property, real estate, machinery and equipment, or intangible assets. The advanced valuation methodologies that they use, combined with the objectivity of their assessments, make them valuable to business owners and buyers alike.

Each of these types of valuation expert has their own preferred methodologies and, to a certain extent, their own subjectivities. It's worth bearing in mind that they also have their own ways of charging you for their services, which mainly come down to convincing you that you could gain a certain amount for your business if you were to sign with them. Please don't mistake their valuations for any kind of guarantee; whatever process they use, it's only their best estimate.

I've worked with many clients who've sold their businesses for more than they thought was possible. This often happens when the right strategic buyer comes along. As an example, I helped an online estate agency sell to a bricks and mortar estate agency chain – the latter desperately needed an online presence and was prepared to pay a premium for a head start in the virtual space. Indeed, the final offer from the successful acquirer was some 30% higher than many of the other offers from interested strategic buyers.

Another key factor in helping you to sell for a great price is to choose the right deal team. This is what we'll look at in the next chapter, when we start Part Two of the book. We're now moving from preparation to the actual sale of your business.

SUMMARY POINTS

- Valuing your business as realistically as possible is critical for deciding whether and when you sell.
- Valuations vary according to when they're done and who does them.
- There are six main valuation methods, each with its own pros and cons.
- The way that you might assess your company's value isn't necessarily the same as the way that buyers would.
- It's important to ask for expert help when valuing your business.

HOW TO VALUE YOUR COMPANY

ACTION POINTS

- Looking at the valuation methods, decide which one or two would be best for your business.
- Research your options in terms of expert valuation assistance and decide which providers you'd like to use.

PART TWO
MAKE THE SALE

7

Your Deal Team: Organising The Support You Need

When you first thought about selling your business, you probably assumed that you'd need some expert advice to get you through the process, such as your accountant and your long-standing solicitor. The truth is that, although these people might be of help, your ideal 'deal team' may well need to be a lot bigger. In my thirty years of experience, I've come to the firm belief that a vital part of your transition from owner to seller requires you to seek specialised knowledge and support from at least four different types of industry expert. They will help you gain the best possible value and experience the smoothest of transactions when you sell your business. These professionals are:

- A broker
- A commercial law firm

- An accountancy firm, and possibly a tax advisor
- A wealth management advisor

There may be others (such as business sale consultants like me) whom you decide to bring in as well, but in this chapter, we'll focus on the above four. I'll explain who they are, what they do, and – when it comes to your broker and lawyer – what to look out for when you're choosing them.

Having helped clients to scale their businesses and ready them for sale, it's not surprising that, as a trusted advisor, I'm frequently asked for recommendations regarding brokers and other elements of the deal team. I'm a great believer that people buy people, and hence encourage my clients to run with a 'beauty parade', where they meet with multiple options before deciding on a deal team member, given how critical a wrong decision could prove. Over many years, I've developed strong, established relationships with multiple brokers, law firms, tax advisors and wealth advisors, and I like to think that I can almost predict who each client will choose based on 'fit' as much as all the other selection factors.

Your broker

This is your deal architect, and they're pivotal. Far from just being a middleman between you and your buyer, they're a strategic partner in navigating the choppy waters of the most important transaction you may ever make in your life. So, what does a broker do? I've broken down their responsibilities into three stages.

Stage 1: Sale preparation

This relates to the first phase of the sale timeline in Chapter 5. In this, your broker:

- Assesses your sale objective and carries out a legal 'health check' of your business
- Researches potential buyers and develops a sale plan
- Produces your information memorandum and teaser document
- Creates a forecast of your future profits, identifying any value-reducing issues and proposing solutions
- Identifies the most suitable industry valuation methodologies
- Begins creating your data room

Stage 2: Marketing your business

This relates to the second and third phases of the sale timeline. In this, your broker:

- Creates a long-list of potential buyers and, with your input, narrows it down to a shorter prospect list
- Sends out your teaser document, following it up and assessing the interested parties

- Asks credible prospects to sign a nondisclosure agreement before giving them the information memorandum
- Answers their initial questions and coaches you to handle meetings with interested parties
- Seeks initial offers

Stage 3: Finalising the deal

This relates to the fourth phase of the overall sale timeline. In this, your broker:

- Negotiates with interested parties who've submitted offers and reviews the best and final ones
- Selects your preferred buyer and negotiates the best deal they can
- Agrees the heads of terms with your lawyers
- Uploads the preferred bidders' information requests into the data room and answers any queries
- Works with your buyers and their lawyers to agree the sale and purchase agreement
- Completes the deal

What to look for in a good broker

In reality, you'll be hiring a firm rather than an individual person, as there are many areas of expertise involved in brokering a deal. It can be hard to know where to start when you've never worked with a sale broker before, so here are some qualities you should look out for.

Industry expertise. They should be able to show that they have a deep understanding of your industry, either because they've sold businesses in it before or because they've researched it before pitching for your business. They should know what deals have gone through recently, who's actively acquiring in your marketplace, and what types of buyers they think might be interested in a business like yours.

Track record. They should have a proven record of brokering successful transactions of a size similar to yours, maybe even within your industry. Just as important is how they've increased the value of those businesses through the sale. I recommend taking the time to talk with some of their previous clients. Ask what went well or badly, and how the broker helped them to overcome any challenges that arose (as they do with every sale). Also, check how many clients they work with at any one time; ideally, you don't want to be part of a production line.

Network and reach. Part of what you're buying in a broker is their network, both local and global, so it's worth digging into the types of buyers they have connections with. For instance, some of the larger brokers may be well connected with big financial buyers, but that doesn't necessarily mean they have a great network of family offices, strategic buyers or high-net-worth individuals. If you're a smaller business, you probably want to go with a broker who has 'ways in' to the latter group.

Internal resources. It's important that your broker has internal staff who can help to maximise your value at exit. Ask them who will be your deal lead and how they'll be supported internally. Your deal lead is the main person to have conversations with interested buyers, and negotiates with them on your behalf. But, given that selling a business is a massive project, it's best if there's also a project manager to co-ordinate everything.

Some brokers also have in-house finance experts who can complement your own accountant's expertise; they know how to present the numbers to make your business attractive to an acquirer. The broker might also have a research team to draw up the long-list of prospects, and a document writer to present the data in the information memorandum and teaser document. Equally important is the marketing team, who are responsible for the messages that go out to prospects via emails and follow-up calls, and sometimes for generating prospects as well.

Communication skills. Explore how your broker will communicate with you and others throughout the process. Will they be discreet with members of your staff whom you don't want to know about the sale yet? Does your deal lead have the interpersonal skills to position your business clearly and persuasively with prospective buyers, and to have constructive conversations with them while negotiating? I've had mixed experiences with deal leads on that front. Selling a business is a people process, so if your broker isn't capable of representing your brand when negotiating on your behalf, you'll have problems.

A competitive fee structure. Brokers charge fees split into two parts. The first is a fixed fee for the planning, research and marketing of your business, and ranges from £15,000 anywhere up to £50,000. The second is a success fee based on a percentage of the final sale, usually between 2.5% and 3.5%. Like most things in life, fees are negotiable. One thing to look out for is when a broker proposes that the success fee is applicable to both the consideration and the cash that's in the business (top tip: none of my clients pay a percentage on the cash).

Your commercial law firm

After your broker, your solicitor is the second most important member of your deal team. For reasons I'll go into later, it will probably be a firm rather than an individual person. In terms of what a good legal firm does, there are three stages.

Stage 1: Legal audit

This relates to the first phase of the sale timeline, and its purpose is to identify any legal risks that may affect the sale before you take it to market. Your legal firm reviews your:

- **Organisational documents:**
  - Articles of incorporation and bylaws
  - Minutes of board meetings and shareholder resolutions
  - Shareholder agreements
- **Contracts and agreements:**
  - Customer, supplier and employee contracts
  - Leases and real estate contracts
- **Intellectual property documentation:**
  - Patents, trademarks and copyrights
  - Licences and royalty agreements
- **Regulatory compliance:**
  - Industry-specific regulations and licensing requirements
  - Environmental permits and assessments
  - Data privacy and security policies and procedures
- **Litigation and legal claims:**
  - Pending and past legal claims, settlements and judgements

Stage 2: Reviewing and negotiating your heads of terms

This relates to the third phase of the sale timeline and is when your solicitor safeguards your interests by negotiating favourable terms, thereby laying the groundwork for a successful transaction. A great commercial legal firm comes into its own not only by strengthening your hand in the negotiation process, but also by reducing the chances of your buyer renegotiating the deal later on. In this stage, your solicitor:

- Reviews your heads of terms to ensure that it's legally compliant and clearly articulated

- Works with you and your broker to assess whether the terms align with your objectives and expectations

- Scrutinises the terms to ensure that they're reasonable and favourable to you

- Carries out a risk assessment to identify any liabilities in the transaction

- Assesses the impact on your legal position, highlighting terms that might give your buyer the opportunity to reduce the price part way through the process or to claim against you after the deal is done

- Negotiates with the buyer's legal team

- Evaluates the enforceability of the terms, ensuring that they make it difficult for a buyer to withdraw from the transaction without a penalty

- Advises you on the legal consequences of accepting or rejecting specific terms

- Once the terms are agreed, finalises the heads of terms and drafts any ancillary documents

Stage 3: Reviewing the sale and purchase agreement

In this step, which correlates with the fourth phase of the sale timeline, the buyer's legal team creates the first draft of the sale and purchase agreement and sends it to your legal team for review. As you navigate this final, crucial stage of the sale process, your solicitor:

- Ensures that the sale and purchase agreement reflects the heads of terms and negotiates with the buyer's legal team

- Scrutinises each provision, clause and annex of the agreement to make sure that there's nothing which is unfair to you or would never work in practice

- Carries out a risk assessment to identify any liabilities associated with the agreement

- If necessary, negotiates with your buyer's legal team to ask for changes to the agreement that better align with your interests

- Ensures that the agreement complies with relevant laws, regulations and contractual obligations

- Evaluates the enforceability of the agreement and advises you on the legal consequences of accepting or rejecting specific terms

- Ensures that you're fully informed of your legal rights and obligations

- Finalises the agreement with your buyer's legal

team and drafts any ancillary agreements or documents needed to formalise the transaction

- Asks you to sign the agreement and seal the deal

What to look for in a good legal firm

You may have a long-standing relationship with a firm of solicitors that's helped you with business and personal matters over the years, and it's always nice to work with someone you trust, but that doesn't necessarily mean they have expertise in mergers and acquisitions. In addition, they might not have the scale you need, as you don't want to be reliant on only one person. What happens if they go on holiday in the middle of the deal, or are swamped with other work? Once the deal is underway, it's all about maintaining momentum.

Most good brokers will have a panel of law firms with whom they've worked in the past and are happy to recommend. It's always worth considering these outfits. Not only do you know that they'll work well with your broker, but they might also offer to carry out the initial legal audit free of charge with a view to being in the box seat when it comes to you picking a practice to carry out the transaction.

Having a practical, get-it-done approach to problem solving is particularly important in a solicitor. When it goes wrong, it goes badly wrong. I've seen situations in which lawyers on both sides seem to forget that they're paid to help their clients and spend a lot of time running up hourly bills by competing for 'top dog' position. The people who lose out are inevitably the buyer and seller.

I suggest you take some recommendations from fellow business owners who have been through the sale process, and also from your broker. You're looking for a practice with strong transactional experience and a team that's large enough to cope with the short timescale that comes with selling a business.

Your accountant and tax advisor

Your broker may have accountancy expertise within the team they put together for you, but you'll probably also need an external accountant to help with the sale. If that accountant offers specialised tax advice as part of their service, that's ideal, but if they don't, you should hire a tax expert separately. Both accountant and tax advisor need to work closely with one another throughout the sale process. For this reason, I've broken down the work that your financial team will do into five areas, each with separate responsibilities for your accountant and tax specialist.

Financial analysis

This takes place during the first phase of the sale timeline.

Accountant's role: To help your broker create your information memorandum by reporting on your company's cash flow projections, assets and liabilities. They also need to be able to share the reconciliations that make up the differences between your management accounts and your annual filings at Companies House. Many of these will be different to the usual ones created by your accountant for tax purposes as they're designed to present your business in the best possible light for a buyer.

Tax advisor's role: There would be nothing more galling than to sell your business for a great sum only to give away a disproportionate amount in tax. A tax advisor can help your broker evaluate the tax implications of the sale, so that together they can create optimisation strategies to minimise your tax exposure and maximise the after-tax proceeds for you.

Financial due diligence

This work takes place during the first phase of the sale timeline.

Accountant's role: To verify the accuracy of the financial information you've given to your broker so that your broker can share it with potential buyers.

Tax advisor's role: To carry out tax due diligence to assess whether you and your business are tax compliant. The aim of this is to spot any tax-related issues before you market your business for sale.

Deal structuring and financial planning

This work takes place during the third phase of the sale timeline.

Accountant's role: If you've decided not to use a broker, your accountant is the person to help you structure the deal in a way that optimises your financial outcomes. They analyse different deal structures to assess the financial implications in terms of taxes, liabilities and cash flow. Normally, however, this area is the responsibility of a broker.

Tax advisor's role: As the deal edges closer to reality, your tax advisor might give you strategic advice on deal structuring (such as tax-deferred exchanges or instalment sales) so as to minimise your tax liabilities.

Financial modelling and forecasting

This work also takes place during the third phase of the sale timeline.

Accountant's role: To develop financial models and forecasts to predict your financial performance post-sale. This could also be carried out by your broker's in-house finance specialist. Given that the sale process can take a year or two, these forecasts can evolve; if you win more business, it would be in your interests for your accountant to update your forecasts and ask buyers to offer more.

Tax advisor's role: To incorporate tax considerations into the accountant's financial modelling and forecasting, helping you to anticipate the tax consequences of different deal scenarios.

Post-sale financial planning

This takes place during the fifth phase of the sale timeline.

Accountant's role: To give you and your broker post-sale support, such as doing your completion accounts.

Tax advisor's role: Together with your wealth management advisor, your tax advisor will provide tax planning and advice, helping you to navigate the tax implications of whatever you decide to do with your money from the sale.

Your wealth management advisor

This is the final piece of the jigsaw. While there's often an overlap between what this person does and the responsibilities of your accountant and tax specialist, a wealth management advisor is the main person to care of your personal, long-term financial future. There are three stages to their work.

Stage 1: Before the sale

This relates to the first phase of the sale timeline, as it's important that you know how much you must sell your business for if you're to have the life you want afterwards. A wealth management advisor can help you to understand this, taking into account your financial goals, attitude to risk and current financial situation.

If you don't have a separate tax advisor, they may also help you to explore tax-efficient ways to structure the sale. Well beforehand, they should also help you to put in place wealth protection strategies to safeguard your assets and mitigate risks.

Stage 2: During the sale

This relates to the fourth phase of the sale timeline. As the sale progresses, your wealth management advisor's focus shifts towards advising you on strategies to safeguard your capital and minimise your expenses during the transition period. This involves helping you to make sure that the deal is structured in a tax-efficient way.

Stage 3: After the sale

This comes during the fifth phase of the sale timeline. After you've sold your business, your wealth management advisor should help you to make the most of your newfound wealth in as tax-efficient a way as possible. It's their job to keep you abreast of market trends, economic developments and investment opportunities so that you can use your new money to make more of the same.

The whole is greater than the sum of its parts

As the industrialist Andrew Carnegie once said, 'Teamwork is the ability to work together toward a common vision.' You need all the parties in your deal team to create a collective focus, working together so that your best interests are kept at the heart of the selling journey. It's in this seamless integration of expertise that a great deal lies.

That's why collating your team isn't only about picking the right people, but also about encouraging them to work together. I suggest bringing them into the same room at the start of the process so that you can explain why you're selling your business, what you aim to achieve with the sale, and how you want everyone to work both individually and collectively. With a high-functioning deal team on your side, you have the best chance of selling your company in a way that maximises the benefits for you.

In the next chapter, we'll look more closely at the role of your deal team, especially that of your broker, when it comes to marketing your business for sale.

SUMMARY POINTS

- To sell your business, you need a broker, a legal firm, an accountant and tax advisor, and a wealth management expert.
- It's important that they work well together so

---

as to make the sale as painless and profitable as possible.

- It's worth spending time choosing people who have the right experience and skills for your needs, and who are willing to collaborate with one another.

8

Marketing Your Business For Sale: How To Attract The Best Offers

N ow that you've primed your company and created your deal team, all you have to do is to put your business on the market and wait for the offers to flood in. I wish that was true, but unfortunately it's not quite that simple. Marketing your business for sale is far more complicated than selling another large asset, such as a house. It involves analysing all the elements that might make it attractive to various types of acquirers, gaining their interest (while at the same time working out if they're someone you want to sell to), and then managing the relationships so that you negotiate the best offers. All while keeping the process confidential.

There's a lot to do, but the good news is that most of it is your broker's job – this is where they earn their fee. You can sell a business without a broker, but you'd be wise to work with one. I advise people on buying companies as well as selling them, and I've often helped clients to buy companies whose owners didn't have professional support. I'm pretty sure that not only did the sellers leave value on the table, but that, if they'd enlisted a broker, it would have paid for itself many times over. If you're thinking you can save money by going it alone, my suggestion is to pause for a moment and consider the opportunity cost. With 65% of businesses on the market failing to sell at all, it makes sense to use the professional expertise available to you.[9]

Assuming that I've convinced you of the benefits of enlisting a decent broker, it's worth knowing what they do to sell your business. This is so that you can support them and give them the time they need to carry out their work. The marketing of a business for sale falls into two phases – preparation and going to market – each of which has its own set of tasks. The rest of this chapter outlines what those tasks are and how they contribute to you receiving a great set of offers.

Preparation

There are some preparatory steps that a successful marketing campaign needs to go through before your business is formally taken to market. The purpose of this is to ensure the sale runs smoothly and that there's minimal opportunity for your future buyer to negotiate the

---

9   Debussy, A, *BizBuySell Insight Report* (BizBuySell, no date), www .bizbuysell.com/insight-report, accessed 13 February 2025

price downwards further down the line. It involves a great deal of planning and analysis, but the work carried out now will pay dividends later in both time and money.

The first three steps of the preparation phase focus on analysing your business, and the last three look outwards to the marketing of it.

Step 1: The financial forecast

You and your broker develop a realistic financial forecast that reflects the likely future performance of your business. This is a critical tool for helping potential buyers to understand what the return on their investment might be. The forecast is made up of:

- Historical financial analysis based on your past financial performance, to identify trends and project future earnings

- Market analysis based on industry trends, market conditions and the competitive landscape, to predict future growth opportunities

- A variety of scenarios based on predicted future revenue, expenses and market conditions

- Revenue projections based on current contracts, customer relationships and market demand

- Expense projections using forecasted operating costs, and fixed and variable expenses, to determine future profitability

- Cash flow projections to show that the business will remain financially healthy

Step 2: The legal audit

All buyers want to be sure there are no skeletons in the cupboard that could be discovered after they've acquired a company, so they will conduct their own legal audit as part of their due diligence after they've made an offer. Anything of concern that they dig up will delay the sale and give them a reason to pay less, which is why your own legal audit at this stage is critical. To this end, your broker typically enlists the support of in-house or third-party legal expertise in order to:

- Examine your contracts with customers, suppliers, employees and other stakeholders, to ensure that they're up to date and legally sound

- Verify that your business adheres to the relevant regulations, employment laws and environmental regulations

- Look into any past or ongoing legal disputes to understand the liabilities involved

- Ensure that all your intellectual property is properly documented and protected

Step 3: The tax audit

As with the legal audit, the purpose of the tax audit is to give your potential buyers the reassurance of knowing that your affairs are in order. It prevents them from using tax concerns as a reason to reduce what they pay for your business and forestalls any delays to the sale process. For this, your broker:

- Reviews your past tax returns to identify any potential issues

- Ensures that your tax liabilities are accounted for and that no outstanding obligations could affect the sale

- Verifies your compliance with all applicable tax laws and regulations

- Works with tax professionals to minimise your tax liabilities related to the sale, such as capital gains tax

Step 4: The potential buyer long-list

We now move from analysing your company's financial and legal situation to exploring who's in the market to acquire it. In this stage, your broker creates a long-list of potential buyers that includes everyone who could possibly be interested in it, with the aim of narrowing it down later. To do this, they extensively research relevant companies, private equity firms and individual investors, and evaluate them based on their strategic goals. Are they actively looking to grow through acquisition? Would your business be a good strategic fit for them? And do they have the financial firepower to make a deal of this size, or are they too small or already overstretched? The broker will also review their track record in terms of acquisitions they've made in the past. Are they experienced in buying companies, and would they be a helpful partner on the selling journey?

At the end of this process, your broker has a long-list of qualified potential buyers who might be interested in, and capable of, acquiring your company. But that doesn't mean you would necessarily want them to approach the whole list. There may be customers or suppliers on there, or other businesses that you wouldn't want to learn your company is up for sale. There might also be a business or two that you'd feel unhappy about entrusting your employees to. It's always your decision, which is why your broker reviews the list with you to gain your approval and make adjustments as necessary.

Step 5: The information memorandum

This is a comprehensive document that ultimately gives interested parties from the long-list of potential buyers the detailed information they need to decide whether they're interested in making an offer (subject to due diligence) to buy your business. To create it, your broker uses the information from your financial, legal and tax audits, and data on your market position and future growth opportunities, to make it as compelling as possible. They want anyone who reads it to see your company as a tempting acquisition opportunity, and this involves working with copywriters and designers to create an impactful communication piece. Your broker can, and often will, tailor it to appeal to different types of buyers.

Step 6: The teaser document

However attractive your broker makes your business look in the information memorandum, there's no getting away from the fact that it's a long document and it will be hard work for a busy entrepreneur to read on spec. What's more, you probably don't want your entire long-list of potential buyers to know that your company is up for sale – it's better only to reveal your identity to those who are seriously interested. That's why your broker extracts the most salient points from the memorandum into a teaser document (sometimes called an executive summary). This is an anonymised synopsis of your business sale opportunity which is designed to pique the interest of potential acquirers. Although it's created after the memorandum, it's sent out beforehand as the first step in the 'go to market' phase.

Go to market

This is when the preparatory work pays off. You have your long-list of potential buyers and your marketing materials, so now it's time for your broker to bring the two together. You could think of this phase as being like a funnel, with the long-list gradually being whittled down to a much shorter and more targeted group of interested parties. By the end, your aim is to have a qualified short-list of best and final offers to choose from, but before you reach that point, there's a number of steps that your broker goes through.

Step 1: Contact the long-list of potential buyers

Your broker's research team contacts the people on the approved long-list, in confidence, to see whether they're interested in making an acquisition in theory. If they receive a favourable response, they send them the teaser document. Remember that the buyers don't know your company's identity yet, your broker is just testing the water.

Step 2: Follow up the teaser document

A few days after sending the teaser document, your broker speaks to the recipients to hear their thoughts. Are they still interested? Do they have any initial questions or concerns that can be addressed? Part of the purpose of this is for your broker to find out how the potential acquirer might fund an acquisition – would it be with their own cash or from money they'd need to raise specially? And if they're a subsidiary company, what does their holding company think? By the end of this step, your broker has a shorter list of interested parties who are both genuinely interested in buying a company like yours and have the financial wherewithal to do so.

Step 3: Assess interested parties for suitability

The qualification of potential buyers doesn't stop at the conversations above. Once your broker knows who's interested, they carry out further background assessments with the aim of disqualifying those who don't appear to have genuine interest or who are just 'tyre kickers'. As they do this, they're working out what's in it for the buyer to acquire your business. Do their strategic goals align with your company's strengths and potential? And do they have both sufficient funds and a successful track record of buying, integrating and growing companies? If not, they might come off the list.

With this assessment done, your broker sends the remaining parties a nondisclosure agreement to sign before issuing them with the full information memorandum. They should also explain the importance of maintaining confidentiality, as this is the first time your potential buyers will be told your company's identity.

Step 4: Follow up the information memorandum

After sending out the memorandum, your broker contacts the recipients to discuss it. The aim here is to further qualify or disqualify people based on their likelihood of making an offer, and to answer any questions they may have. By the end of this step, the ever-smaller pool of potential buyers is limited to those who are well informed and still engaged with the process.

Step 5: Set the timeline

Up to this point, the timeline of the sale hasn't been a central part of the process, but now your broker wants to create a sense of urgency so that the sale remains on track. They establish a timeline for submitting first-round offers and give the interested parties guidance on the format and content so that they're easy to compare. Part of your broker's purpose here is also to encourage more conversations and answer more questions, so as to help potential buyers decide whether or not to stay involved.

Step 6: Arrange face-to-face meetings between you and the potential buyers

This is where you come in. Now that your broker has a short-list of interested potential acquirers who have all the information they need, the next step is for you to meet them face-to-face (or by video or phone call). If they're still interested after one meeting, they'll probably want a series of conversations so as to satisfy the needs of various people in their buying teams.

These meetings are a crucial part of your potential buyers' decision-making process because they allow them to gain a deeper understanding of you, your business and your vision for it. In turn, they enable you to build trust and rapport with them. Making the right impression is important, and to help you with this, your broker will spend a lot of time coaching you in how to handle the meetings. They will advise you on what you can and can't say, and how to disclose just enough information to get buyers excited without giving away too much. This coaching can include role-playing as a way of practising how to answer common questions, put across the key strengths of your business, and come across as honest and professional.

Step 7: Gather first-round offers

Off the back of these meetings, first-round offers come in. Exciting times! Your broker reviews them to ensure that they include all the right information, which might involve going back to some potential buyers to clarify the odd point (you'd be amazed at how often initial offers are unclear or misleading). They then create a summary of all the offers for easy comparison.

Step 8: Review first-round offers with you

Remember when we looked at the role of your broker as a member of your deal team, and saw that one of the things you agreed with them at the start is what your ideal offer would look like? This is where that decision comes into play. While your broker is comparing the offers, they will also measure them against the criteria you set. In fact, any decent broker should tell potential buyers what these criteria are early in the process. Of course, buyers do what suits them, but given that it's a competitive process, most would think carefully before tabling an offer that flies in the face of what you want. Your broker's role is to advise you on which offers tick all the boxes, which ones warrant further conversations, and which ones will never meet your expectations.

Step 9: Invite best and final offers

No broker ever accepts an initial offer as final, even if it's the only one they receive (something that they'd never tell the potential acquirer in any case, as they want to encourage an improved offer). Instead, they encourage the buyer to better it: 'Thanks for your first-round offer, it's definitely attracted the seller's interest. However, I think you may have undervalued the growth potential in this business. Would you mind explaining how you've come to your valuation? And then, would you perhaps have another think about what your best and final offer would be?'

I had a client in the facilities management industry who sold his business to an overseas acquirer just over two years ago. Despite an extensive marketing effort by their broker, the Covid-19 pandemic had definitely dampened market enthusiasm at the time, and the acquirer was in fact the only party to make an offer. Through careful positioning by the broker, the overseas party was persuaded to improve their offer not once, but twice, given that they were of the belief that they were in a competitive situation. The net result was that the overseas acquirer ended up paying nearly 40% more than their initial offer. A great example of a broker using all of their guile and experience, and an even greater result for the seller!

This is how, in the final step of the marketing process,

your most promising potential buyers are encouraged to put forward their strongest bids. Your broker gives them a deadline to keep momentum going and communicates any additional expectations or requirements. The result, hopefully, is a great set of proposals for your business that not only offer a high purchase price, but also take into account the deal structure that's important to you. From this, you select your preferred offer, and what happens next is the subject of the following chapter.

SUMMARY POINTS

- When marketing your business for sale, there's a lot more preparation work to be done than you might think.
- This preparation is designed to keep the sale running smoothly and prevent potential buyers from renegotiating their offers later in the process.
- Critical to marketing your business is fostering a sense of urgency and competition between interested parties so that they're encouraged to keep improving their offers.
- While the marketing process is largely down to your broker, you have an important role to play in winning over potential buyers during your meetings with them.

9

The Offer: Evaluating And Negotiating The Deal

Let me introduce you to Bridget and Andrew. Bridget is the founder of a subscription-based household cleaning products company that she launched seven years ago and recently pushed into profit. Andrew is the owner of a small chain of restaurants that went through some hard times during Covid, but which has emerged stronger and more resilient since. Both entrepreneurs have selected their preferred offers for their companies, but while the top-line figures in the deals are the same, they're structured differently.

Bridget has been offered £8 million for her company, with £5 million up front and the remaining £3 million as two equal deferred payments over the next two years, regardless of business performance. She's happy with the overall price and likes the certainty of knowing what she'll receive in the future, but has a niggling concern that, given her business is now growing strongly and is predicted to do even better, her instalments might be higher if they were linked to future growth. At the same time, however, she's relieved that her buyer only wants her to stay on for six months after the sale, as she has another business opportunity to move on to. Given that she'll receive the deferred payments no matter how her business performs, this also allays any concern that she won't be around for long enough to make sure it grows as expected. On balance, therefore, she decides that this is the best deal for her.

Andrew has a different dilemma. Like Bridget, he's also been offered £8 million for his company, with £5 million up front and the remaining £3 million in two instalments over the next two years. But his instalments are contingent on his business' future performance (commonly known as a 'contingent earnout', or 'contingent consideration'). His market can be volatile, which means that it's far from certain whether he'll receive any or all of the £3 million, and, on top of that, he has capital gains tax to consider. Under current UK tax law, you have to pay tax on the total sale value of your company (in Andrew's case, £8 million) even if some of the payment is due in future years. If he doesn't receive the contingent payments, he can claim that element of his tax back, but that will, of course, take time.

Andrew wants to pay off the mortgage on his million-pound house and has plans to buy a property abroad this year, so the combination of the tax burden and the potential nonpayment of his contingent instalments is a concern. On the other hand, given that his buyer wants him to stay on for two years, he can turn this to his advantage if he negotiates an autonomous leadership role that enables him to keep his restaurants on track. On top of that, he'll also receive a higher contingent payment if the business performs better than expected – that would really sweeten the pill.

Bridget and Andrew's stories illustrate what lies beneath the headline numbers of a consideration (that's business jargon for 'offer'). There are always additional terms and conditions to consider as well. Even if it's a knockout deal, your broker will probably want to find ways to improve it – and this won't be restricted to the overall sale price. It might include altering your earnout period, the structure of the payments, the way that your business debt is calculated and accounted for, whether your buyer acquires your whole company or only part of it, noncompete clauses that restrict what you do after the sale, and other factors.

This is why understanding all the components of an offer is critically important. In my experience, it's not necessarily the highest price that wins, but a combination of financial numbers and terms. It takes time and knowledge to balance this out, particularly if you're a first-time seller, which is why I'll lead you through all the aspects of a consideration that you need to be aware of.

Key terminology

Whatever stage an offer is at – initial, or best and final – it will contain a number of components, all of which you need to understand and then compare with the ideal offer that you decided on at the start. Here are the main terms that you'll come across, which I'll explain in more detail later on.

- **Purchase price:** The entire amount the buyer is willing to pay for your business (the 'total consideration'). How does this compare to your valuation and envisaged minimum sale price?

- **Cash up front:** The portion of the purchase price paid at closing and the amount to be deferred. Is this your preferred balance?

- **Taxes:** The tax implications of the sale for both parties. Are these acceptable to you?

- **Earnouts:** Payments contingent on the business achieving certain performance targets post-sale. This involves a level of risk – is it within your tolerance limit?

- **Escrow:** Funds held in escrow to cover any potential post-sale liabilities. Can you afford this?

- **Warranties:** Assurances demanded from you about your business' condition and operations. Are you willing to provide them?

- **Indemnities:** Provisions you make for compensating your buyer in case you breach your warranties. Do they seem reasonable to you?

- **Timings:** Your buyer's schedule for completing the transaction. Does it fit with your plans?

What you want versus what your buyer wants

Given that you're now moving into more intensive negotiations, it's worth understanding how your objectives may differ from those of your seller. This helps you to see things from their point of view and to come up with an agreement that you're both happy with. Here are the areas in which you're most likely to have opposing objectives.

The purchase price

This is the most obvious one. You're aiming for the highest possible figure so as to maximise the return on your investment, whereas your buyer (surprise, surprise) seeks what they see as a fair price, which will often be lower – especially considering that they're taking on risk.

The proportion of cash paid up front

You will probably prefer a high proportion of cash up front so that it's in the bank and available for whatever you want to spend it on. This also reduces the risk of you not receiving the instalments due to your business not meeting its targets or your buyer having financial problems. For these reasons, I recommend that you ask for at least 65% to 75% of the total consideration up front. Your buyer, on the other hand, prefers to minimise their initial cash outlay, using deferred payments to manage their cash flow and, if the deal has a contingent element, incentivise you to grow the business in the future.

Taxes

I mentioned the personal tax liability when you sell a business earlier on. Your aim is to reduce this as much as possible through managing your capital gains treatment, whereas your buyer is more interested in maximising their own tax efficiency. They will often do this through amortisation of their purchased assets or through other tax strategies, such as by topping up pension contributions with surplus cash.

Earnouts

An earnout is when your instalments are contingent on business performance. You may prefer guaranteed deferred payments over contingent ones, in that they're not reliant on a future that you can no longer fully control because you no longer own the business. Your buyer, however, wants to mitigate the risk of buying a company whose performance can't be guaranteed. By making their payments contingent, they potentially only pay all of the contingent amounts if you hit or exceed the growth or profits thresholds. Conversely, if you're confident in the growth and have negotiated, with your broker, potential increases in contingent amounts should you exceed the targets, there could well be a win-win for both parties.

Escrow

It's normal for buyers to hold back some money from the initial cash payout until the completion accounts are done – sometimes as much as 5–10%. You want to minimise the amount held in escrow, so that not only can you access the full proceeds as quickly as possible, but also avoid escrow fees, which it's normal for the seller to pay and which can run into thousands of pounds. Your buyer sees it differently, however. They prefer a large escrow so as to protect them against unforeseen liabilities and ensure your compliance with the sale terms.

Warranties

These are guarantees you make about the financial and legal health of your business. You want to limit the scope and duration of the warranties so as to reduce your future liabilities, but your buyer's interest lies in demanding extensive warranties to protect them from misrepresentations.

Indemnities

These are promises you make to compensate your buyer should you break any of your warranties. Your aim is to cap your indemnities so as to avoid paying out large sums in the future, whereas your buyer wants broad indemnity provisions to safeguard them against any post-sale issues.

Factors influencing how hard you can negotiate

While you're working out which terms you're happy to accept and which ones you want to drive a hard bargain on, it's worth understanding the factors that have an impact on the strength of your position as a negotiator. The main ones are:

- **Business valuation:** If your buyer values your business highly, this gives you the opportunity to drive harder negotiations.

- **Market conditions:** The economic climate and industry trends affect your leverage.

- **The type of buyer:** For instance, a strategic buyer may offer a high price if there are synergies they can exploit, while a financial buyer is likely to focus on return on investment in the longer term.

- **The competition:** If you receive multiple quality offers, this gives you the chance to drive up the sale price and ask for better terms.

- **Your time frame:** An urgency to sell can weaken your negotiating position.

The heads of terms agreement

Once you and your broker have negotiated the initial offers, received best and final offers and selected one you are most interested in, you move into a period of exclusivity with that one potential buyer in which they draw up the heads of terms agreement. This document is a preliminary agreement outlining the main terms of the transaction. It isn't legally binding, but it does map out the key points that will be fleshed out in the much longer sale agreement that comes afterwards.

Key elements of the heads of terms

Here are the points you and your legal team should look out for in this important document:

- **Purchase price and payment structure:** These clarify the total consideration and how it will be paid (cash, stock and earnouts).
- **Conditions to close:** These are the criteria that must be satisfied before the transaction can be finalised.
- **Exclusivity period:** This gives your buyer a period to carry out their due diligence without competition from other buyers, and sets the timeline both parties need to work to.

- **Confidentiality:** This ensures that both parties keep the transaction details private.

Negotiating the heads of terms

Despite you and your buyer having agreed on the structure of the deal, when their lawyers get involved in drawing up the heads of terms, it's not unusual for new clauses to be slipped in that aren't particularly favourable to you. These need to be questioned and challenged by your broker and legal team. The smoothest deals are always the ones in which the major points of contention are dealt with at this stage, before the full sale agreement is produced. A well-negotiated heads of terms sets a positive tone for the processes to come and reduces the likelihood of disputes.

To negotiate the heads of terms, you begin by having informal discussions with your acquirer to gauge your alignment on the major points, such as price, payment structure and timelines. The legal advisors for both parties then review the document, making sure that any legal and tax implications are also addressed. They will probably go back and forth a few times while they agree the final points, then both parties sign the document. This signals your intention to proceed.

By this stage, you've potentially spent a lot of money on lawyers and other experts, and you don't want to be left out of pocket if your buyer pulls out for some reason. I remember a business I negotiated to buy early in my career, when I didn't know what I do now. We'd agreed the heads of terms, but on the day that we were due to sign the full sale contract, the seller decided not to sell after all. I was left £40,000 out of pocket and vowed I'd never be caught out like that again. For this reason, I suggest that you ask for one binding term in the heads of terms, which is that if the buyer abandons the purchase for any reason other than material changes arising during due diligence, they indemnify you against your legal costs.

Things to take into account

I've walked you through the process of analysing and negotiating your preferred offer, but while you're doing that, there are some factors you need to be aware of if you're not to be caught off guard. Sometimes, it's simply a matter of knowing what certain terms mean or what the implications are for you. What follows is an explanation of these factors and how they could have an impact on your sale.

Share sale versus asset sale

A share sale is when your buyer acquires all the shares in your company and everything that goes with them, for instance your brand, equipment and contracts. In other words, the whole lot. An asset sale is when you sell only parts of your business, such as your machinery, customer database or real estate.

An example of an asset sale comes from a client of mine, Sean, who owned a company that had two parts to it. One was the original business, which was a large and well-respected English language school, and the other was a spin-off comprising a group of rental houses that he used to accommodate students visiting from abroad. His buyer, a strategic acquirer, was initially interested in buying Sean's entire company as a share sale transaction, but later decided that he was only interested in the language school as it was the element that best fitted with their existing business. In addition to the school building itself, they acquired the staff, customer database and brand. Sean was happy with that, as he was able to sell the houses to another buyer.

In a **share sale**, there are pros and cons for both you and your buyer:

Pros for you: It's a simpler process than an asset sale and might give you the opportunity to reduce your capital gains tax. That's because asset sales can trigger different types of taxes, such as income tax on recaptured depreciation, and these can complicate the transaction.

Cons for you: Because your buyer assumes all your liabilities, it can lower the price they're willing to offer.

Pros for your buyer: A share purchase gives them continuity of business operations and is often simpler from a regulatory standpoint.

Cons for your buyer: They take on aspects of your business that may increase their risk.

Likewise, in an **asset sale**, there are also pros and cons for both parties:

Pros for you: You can retain specific parts of your company if you want to, which gives you more control.

Cons for you: In an asset sale, the buyer selects specific assets and liabilities they want to purchase, which entails identifying, valuing and transferring each asset and liability individually. This process is often more complex because it involves detailed negotiations and legal documentation for each item being transferred.

Pros for your buyer: They can be selective about what parts of your business they take on.

Cons for your buyer: They might have to re-value your assets, and also go through a more complex transfer process when the sale is done.

Deferred versus contingent consideration (earnout)

You met these concepts earlier in the stories of Bridget and Andrew, but it's worth going into more detail here. A deferred consideration is when your buyer pays part of the purchase price over time, usually in fixed instalments. A contingent consideration (or earnout) is when your buyer pays the remainder of the agreed purchase price over time, based on your business achieving specific performance targets.

With **deferred payments**, there are pros and cons for both you and your buyer:

Pros for you: They allow you additional income over time, which can reduce or spread out your tax burden if instalments fall within different tax years.

Cons for you: Your access to the money is delayed, and you also run the risk that your buyer defaults on the payments.

Pros for your buyer: They can better manage their cash flow, and potentially borrow less money if they're funding the deal through debt financing.

Cons for your buyer: They make for more complex deal structures, which can lead to interest charges and extra legal costs.

Likewise, **contingent earnout payments** have pros and cons for both you and your buyer:

Pros for you: There's the potential to receive higher payments if you exceed your targets.

Cons for you: You might not meet the targets, which makes for some uncertainty about your future payouts. What's more, when you don't own your company anymore and are perhaps not working in it full-time, you're not in such a good position to make sure that you reach your targets. This opens the way for disputes with your buyer if the subject isn't covered in intricate detail in the sale and purchase agreement.

Pros for your buyer: Contingent payments reduce their upfront risk and incentivise you to ensure not only a smooth transition, but excellent business performance after the sale.

Cons for your buyer: They're complex to structure and monitor, and any disputes are likely to be as difficult for them to handle as they are for you.

Dealing with debt at closing

Deals are typically done on a debt-free basis, where you pay off your debts before the sale or compensate your buyer for the debt so that they can pay it off themselves. Here, we look at how that works in terms of how the offer is negotiated and closed.

The first thing to be aware of is that your buyer doesn't necessarily require all your debts to be paid up when you complete the transaction. Suppose you're an electrical contractor with twelve leased vans on the road. On your books, the leases are expressed as debt, and it's possible that your buyer may insist that they're paid off. But with leasing, it's common for buyers to see that kind of debt simply as a cost of doing business.

On the other hand, if you have £70,000 worth of business loans outstanding and owe £20,000 of corporation tax that isn't yet due, your buyer will almost always require that you either pay these off using the sale proceeds or leave behind an equivalent amount for the buyer to pay them. These are called 'closing adjustments' and are included in your completion accounts, with funds set aside in the escrow to cover any unforeseen liabilities that your buyer discovers post-closing.

Handover or consultancy periods

These ensure a smooth transition of your business oper-ations and relationships, so as to maintain continuity with your clients and employees. These sometimes require you to stay on for a year or two as a consultant or advisor, or as an employee with a significant role in the business. In all the years I've been helping people to sell their companies, I've never met an owner who wants to stay on, but it's rare that they get their wish. It's therefore probable that you'll need to commit your-self to a handover in one form or another.

The question is, what sort of handover or consul-tancy will you agree to? It might be that you've already established an amazing management team that can run your company without you, in which case you proba-bly won't be required for long. But if you're still active in your business, your buyer is likely to want to hold onto you so they have access to your expertise and can ensure that you can help with any problems that arise in the transition. This could be for anything from six months to two years.

The advantage to you of staying on is that, if you've agreed to a contingent consideration, you'll probably want to be around to influence your revenue and profit growth. If this is the case, include the nature of your role in your negotiations – otherwise, what are you signing up to? The worst-case scenario would be for your income to be dependent on hitting targets when you don't have enough autonomy within the new busi-ness to achieve them.

In the case of a deferred consideration in which the seller is contracted to stay on for a year, their involvement doesn't always last that long. The buyer says, 'We're six months into the transition and we think we've got this sussed. You don't really need to be here anymore, so we'll release you with the caveat that, if anything goes horribly wrong, you'll be there to help.' They may actually prefer to run things without you, just like you might do if you bought a business where the previous owner was still in place.

Noncompete clauses

Maybe you make so much money from your sale that you never need to work again. If so, that's great, but it doesn't mean you'll necessarily want to exit the business world entirely. You might be thinking of working in another company in the same field, either in terms of sector or geography; this could be as an owner or as an employee or consultant. Your buyer, however, may have other ideas. They will want to protect their interests and the assets that they've just acquired by preventing you from working in competition with them, especially given your inside knowledge. Nor will they relish the thought of you attracting your previous clients or employees away. This is where noncompete clauses come in.

There's often quite a bit of negotiation around noncompete clauses, ranging from whether you can do any work at all for a period of time, to whether you can do certain work that doesn't directly compete with your new owner. The question is, what do you and your buyer each see as 'competing'? Would you be allowed to work with a supplier of the business you've just sold, for instance? Or a customer? Or to set up a new company in the same geographical area? Different buyers have different views, so it's important to pin this down. Key issues that need to be clarified include the length of time for the noncompete clause, the geographic scope, and the types of activities that you're not allowed to engage in. From your perspective, it's worth bearing in mind that noncompete clauses can only be enforceable if they're reasonable, and that you can also leverage any noncompete restrictions as a way of increasing your sale price.

By the end of this phase of the sale process, you'll have negotiated the heads of terms to both your and your buyer's satisfaction and are now set to move on to the next step. This is due diligence, which is your buyer's process of checking that everything you've claimed about your business is actually true. As you can imagine, there's much to cover before the sale is in the bag, so this is what we'll look at in the next chapter.

SUMMARY POINTS

- It's an exciting moment when you receive a selection of offers and settle on your favourite, but the headline figures are only part of the story.

- The terms of the offer are also important, such as deferred or contingent payments, warranties, timings and tax implications.
- It's important to understand what your buyer wants as well as what you want if you're to negotiate a deal that everyone is happy with.
- The heads of terms is the document that summarises the main points of the sale, and forms the basis of the full sale agreement.
- Other aspects of the offer to consider are whether it's a share or asset sale, how you handle debt at closing, the handover period you agree to, and any noncompete clauses.

10

Due Diligence: What To Expect From Your Buyer

The due diligence process is your potential buyer's final chance to become completely confident that your business is as you've said it is. If, at this stage, they discover anything that gives them cause for concern, they may renegotiate their offer or even walk away altogether. Even minor renegotiations can result in you losing a chunk of value, and let's not forget the hourly rates of your legal and accounting teams, who will have extra work to do. I've heard of many deals that have gone wrong in this way, which is why I always ensure my clients have done thorough preparatory work before we get to this stage.

Now is when the work you put into preparing for the sale pays off, as gathering the financial, operational, legal and other documentation you need for due diligence can take an eternity. Where are all your insurance documents? If you're including your office building in the sale, where's the original planning permission (plus the secondary permission for the solar panels you installed)? Where are your employee and customer contracts? What about the market analysis you carried out a few months ago – is it up to date? If you have everything to hand, you'll avoid delays and keep the momentum going.

Let's recap on where we've got to. You've chosen your preferred buyer and have probably entered into a period of exclusivity while you both sign the heads of terms. The next step is for your buyer's legal team to submit a full due diligence request. This document is long and granular, but it's broken down into numbered sections to make it easier to navigate. Its purpose for your acquirer is two-fold: to check that the things you've said about your business in the information memorandum stand up to scrutiny, and to help them think about how they'll run your business when they take over the reins.

To help you submit answers to the many questions posed by the due diligence request, your buyer's legal team creates a data room. This is a secure online environment to which you, and anyone in your business you authorise, can upload the documentation they're asking for. Your acquirer and their various teams, such as their legal and financial support, are also able to access the room, which keeps the flow of communication smooth and straightforward.

The purpose of this chapter is to tell you what

happens during due diligence so that you're prepared for it. I'll cover the four main areas, which are:

- Financial
- Operational
- Legal
- Other

As you read through them, you'll see that they relate back to the ten drivers of business value that we explored in Chapter 2. During due diligence, your buyer is seeking hard evidence of your company fulfilling those drivers. Does your documentation reassure them on each front, or are there holes and unexpected weaknesses in what you submit to them? This is when you'll find out for sure.

As additional help with getting prepared, you can find a checklist of all the information that you'll be asked to provide at www.chalkhillblue.org/ddchecklist.

Financial due diligence

You've already provided top-line numbers to show that your business is a sound financial investment, but it's during due diligence that your acquirer seeks to validate your claims by drilling down into the details. Their main concern is to understand whether your company's financial future really is as positive as you've said it is.

Financial statements review

Because your historical financial performance is a primary driver of the value of your business, your buyer will scrutinise your past three to five years of income statements, balance sheets and cash flow statements. They will focus on revenue consistency, size of expenses and profits, and cash flows. If your statements are unaudited, they may request an audit to ensure their accuracy.

Profitability analysis

Your buyer needs to know that you have high-quality, sustainable earnings, preferably driven by recurring and predictable revenue streams. To this end, they will analyse your gross margins to assess your cost control and pricing strategies, identify any inefficiencies in your operating expenses, and evaluate your overall profitability so as to understand your business' earning potential.

Cash flow analysis

A strong, positive cash flow is critical, as it indicates whether your business can generate sufficient cash to sustain itself and support growth. Your buyer will review the cash flows from your operations to see whether they generate enough money, and assesses the cash that's available after any spending on growth

WHAT TO EXPECT FROM YOUR BUYER

activities, debt repayments and dividends. They'll also ensure that your cash flow projections are achievable.

Revenue analysis

If your company has the potential to grow, and has a strong sales pipeline and diverse revenue streams, this makes it attractive to a buyer. Your acquirer will want to validate whether the growth potential statements in your information memorandum stack up by examining your revenue by product, service, customer segment and region. They'll also review your most important customer contracts to see how stable and long-term they are, and analyse your future revenue prospects.

Tax compliance

This is about risk management, as your buyer doesn't want to acquire a company that might have hidden tax liabilities. To this end, they'll scrutinise your tax returns for the past three to five years, identifying any outstanding liabilities or disputes, and ensuring that your tax planning strategies are legitimate and realistic.

Operational due diligence

Your buyer will be keen to ensure that they can pick up your business and run with it after they acquire it. This means checking that your strategic plans, organisational structure, processes, supply chain and customer relationships are as you described them in your information memorandum.

Business model and strategy

A scalable and sustainable business model is what your buyer is looking for, so they assess the information you've given them about your business model, including your revenue streams, cost structure and value proposition. They'll also review your strategic plans so that they can understand how you plan for the business to grow, and so they can identify the challenges that might stand in the way of that growth. Even if they plan to change your strategy in favour of their own after the acquisition, they still need to validate it against their own plans.

Organisational structure

The quality of your management team and key employees is critical to your buyer, as strong leadership and a capable workforce are what will make your strategy succeed in real life. By reviewing your organisational chart and staff records, they can understand your reporting lines and assess the qualifications and experience of your most important people. Part of this process involves scrutinising your employment contracts to see whether your key employees can be retained after the acquisition. Depending on the type of buyer, they may not intend to keep all your business functions, planning instead to merge some of them with their own, so this part of due diligence helps them with their decision-making.

Operational processes

If you have efficient operational processes, these help to reduce costs and increase profitability, so your buyer will want to see what your operations look like in detail. To this end, they'll review your documentation of key processes, including those in production, procurement and logistics. Operational key performance indicators are also of interest to them, as are your technology systems such as your customer relationship or project management platforms. Part of the purpose of this is for your buyer to start thinking about whether there's duplication with their own software or processes, and what they might do about it.

Supply chain

A robust supply chain helps your buyer to ensure continuity of operations when your business transfers to them, which makes the purchase a less risky proposition. That's why they'll review the terms and conditions in your supplier contracts and identify any risks in your supply chain, such as over-reliance on certain companies or geopolitical uncertainty. Your buyer will also analyse your inventory levels and supplier turnover rates to see whether your management practices are sound in this area.

Customer relationships

Just as your buyer is keen to see that your business isn't reliant on too few suppliers, they will also want to see that you have a loyal and varied customer base. For this reason, they'll analyse your customer concentration levels and your customer satisfaction surveys and retention rates, so they can be confident that your customers won't leave after the business transfer. They might even ask to meet your key customers to learn what they have to say about you.

Legal due diligence

This part of due diligence is primarily about risk assessment for your buyer, and it's another area where your preparatory work will pay off. You may be confident that your business is legally sound, but do you have all the right documents in one place? Suppose you have a number of shareholders, for instance – do you have shareholder agreements drawn up and easily accessed, or did you skip over that step because it didn't seem important at the time? Here's where you show your hand.

Corporate structure

A well-defined corporate structure reduces legal risks for your buyer and ensures a smooth transition of ownership. To this end, your buyer will review your articles of incorporation, bylaws, shareholder agreements and minutes of board meetings. They'll also ask for evidence of your ownership structure and of any outstanding equity interests or options.

Regulatory compliance

Your buyer doesn't want to take on a business that's not compliant with industry regulations and standards, as that could expose them to legal challenges in the future. Depending on what kind of work you do, this area may be more or less relevant. For instance, you might produce products that have to meet certain standards or you might run a franchise business that can only operate in a specific area. Your buyer will review your filings and correspondence with regulatory authorities and ensure that you have all the necessary licences and permits. They'll also assess whether you have effective compliance policies to ensure that the rules have been kept in reality.

Intellectual property (IP)

This is an important area of value for a business, so your buyer will want to see your related documentation to reassure themselves that you own what you say you do. They'll carry out an IP asset inventory, including your patents, trademarks, copyrights and trade secrets. They'll also verify that you own, and have registered, your IP assets, and identify any potential IP infringements or disputes that could cause them problems in the future.

Contracts and agreements

This relates to your agreements with customers, suppliers, partners and employees, as they all have an impact on your company's value. Your buyer will review your major contracts to understand your rights and obligations, identify risks such as termination clauses or change of control provisions, and review any ongoing litigation that could expose them to risk.

Environmental and social governance

It depends partly on the nature of your business, but strong environmental and social governance practices are increasingly important to buyers as they can enhance your company's reputation and therefore its value. Your buyer will therefore review your environmental impact assessments and compliance with regulations and industry standards, as well as any social responsibility initiatives that you may have put in place.

Other aspects of due diligence

While the financial, operational and legal aspects of due diligence are important, they're not the only areas your buyer will look at. There's a collection of others that are also critical, which I'll detail here.

Market and industry analysis

When you created your information memorandum, you probably painted a bright picture of your company's market and potential for growth, so now's when your buyer validates your claims. They'll assess your company's market position relative to its competitors, analyse industry trends and their potential impact on your business, and evaluate the competitive landscape.

They're looking for industry and market data around these areas and will also ask if you know of any issues that are likely to affect the future performance of your business. A client of mine, David, sold a business that worked with the construction industry helping contractors to reclaim tax. While we were in the process of preparing his company for sale, the government started up a working party to investigate whether the construction tax laws should be changed. This posed a major threat to David's market. He declared this in his information memorandum, but if he hadn't, his buyer would (or should) have discovered it during due diligence.

Real estate and physical assets

The importance of this depends on your business and the assets it has. If you have plant and machinery, or offices and warehouses, these can form a key part of your company's value and so are of interest to your buyer. Any acquirer wants to be sure that your assets have been priced fairly and that they're in good condition, so they'll carry out inspections of your facilities and have them valued. They'll also read your lease agreements with a view to unearthing any terms and obligations that might put their investment at risk. Given that due diligence in this area is about valuing and inspecting assets for defects, it can take time.

As an example, one of my clients has recently concluded the purchase of a business in the north of England, where the seller had a long lease on their existing premises. However, in the midst of due diligence, it was ascertained that the lease contained particularly vague dilapidation clauses. The net result was that this one small element of due diligence delayed the completion of the purchase by nearly two months while the landlord clarified their expectations and adjusted the lease to satisfy our client and their lawyers.

Technology and innovation

If your business has developed advanced technologies or has strong innovation capabilities, this can form a significant part of its value. Your buyer will therefore spend time evaluating your tech infrastructure and whether your research and development claims are robust. Equally, they'll be looking to the future – they'll want to feel comfortable that there is an upside to what you have in development right now, and that you have a healthy innovation pipeline.

Employee relations and culture

It's all well and good inspecting your organisational chart, but your buyer will also want to get under the skin of your company and see what its culture is like. That's because a strong, positive culture boosts employee satisfaction and retention, and ultimately makes your business more valuable. This can be a difficult area to analyse on paper, but your employee satisfaction surveys, initiatives aimed at maintaining a positive culture, and staff turnover rates will all be scrutinised. Equally, due diligence looks to understand what, if any, performance issues, disciplinary or grievance procedures, and health and safety issues, might be present in your company.

Contingent liabilities and risk management

As with legal due diligence, this is primarily about risk assessment. Your buyer will want to ensure that your business is protected against unforeseen liabilities, but only in a way that enhances its value. My wife and I once bought a business that had been paying £15,000 a year for insurance, but when we looked into it, the insurance didn't cover half the risks it had been bought for. On the surface, it was well protected, but in practice, it wasn't. To this end, your buyer will review your insurance policies to check that your cover is adequate and to identify any liabilities that could affect your business. They'll also assess your risk mitigation strategies.

This due diligence process can be time consuming and frustrating, although much less so if you've done the preparation work up front. Once you've passed this hurdle, you're well on the way to negotiating and signing the sale and purchase agreement. This is what we'll look at next.

SUMMARY POINTS

- The main purpose of due diligence is for your potential buyer to validate whether what you've told them about your business is correct.
- It's a critical part of the sale process because if it doesn't go well, it can cause your offer to be renegotiated or even abandoned.
- The main areas for your buyer to focus on are financial, operational and legal.
- If you prepare the documentation before you put your business on the market, it eases the pain of due diligence considerably.

11

Completion: Navigating The Sale And Purchase Agreement

You've travelled a long way on your exit journey and you're now within touching distance of your destination. After agreeing the heads of terms and going through the gruelling process of due diligence, it's time to complete the final legal step: the negotiation and signing of the sale and purchase agreement (SPA).

Before you sign on the dotted line, there's a lot to understand about the complex document that is the SPA. It's important to know what the various terms mean and how to navigate potentially difficult conversations around areas such as restrictive covenants and warranties. While the heads of terms is only a few pages long, the SPA can comfortably be up to 100 pages – sometimes more, with appendices. At first glance, and especially if you're a first-time seller, it can be a daunting document (fortunately made manageable by your legal team, who are the ones to review it and recommend any changes to you).

By this point, you may well be impatient to put the sale to bed and get on with your life, but I encourage you not to rush. You'll have a long time for regrets if you end up agreeing to things that cost you dearly, either financially or in terms of your post-sale lifestyle. You don't want to discover that, in three years' time, an onerous warranty returns to haunt you, or that you've committed yourself to years of consultancy work without understanding the full implications.

To help you navigate the SPA, I'll start by explaining the various legal terms. Then I'll point out the areas that you're most likely to need to pay attention to so that you can filter the document according to your needs. Finally, I'll cover what happens before you finish the deal.

Understanding the terms used in an SPA

The SPA is a comprehensive document that formalises the sale of your business. It covers all aspects of the transaction and ensures that you and your buyer are clear about who receives what and under what conditions. Here are the key components and terms, and what they mean for you.

Purchase price and payment terms

Purchase price: This is the total consideration for your business, including whether the sum is paid in one go or through structured payments over time.

Payment terms: These cover the timings of payments and the conditions attached to them, such as whether they're dependent on business performance. They also include the form of payment, for instance cash, stock or a combination of both.

Assets and liabilities

Assets: A list of the assets that you're transferring, both tangible (such as equipment and stock) and intangible (such as intellectual property and customer contracts).

Liabilities: There may be a specification about which liabilities your buyer will take on and which will remain with you. For instance, your buyer may well want you to pay off outstanding loans, bonuses, and VAT and corporation tax liabilities, while perhaps agreeing to continue funding existing motor and plant leasing costs themselves.

Representations and warranties

Representations: These are the statements of fact that you're making about your business, covering the key areas of finance, operations and legal compliance. For example, that the last three years' accounts have been filed with the appropriate authorities on time, and that you're not aware of any pending legal claims.

Warranties: These are promises made by you that certain conditions are true. They protect your buyer from uncovering undisclosed problems in the future, with the view that, if that happens, they may invoke indemnities (see below).

Indemnities

These are provisions that require one party to compensate the other for specific losses arising after the sale. They typically relate to breaches of representations or warranties.

Restrictive covenants

Noncompete clauses: These prevent you from starting or joining a competing business for a certain period of time, or within a specific geographic area.

Nonsolicitation clauses: These prevent you from approaching your company's customers, suppliers or employees after you've sold it, which you might want to do if you were to set up a new venture.

We'll look a little closer at restrictive covenants in a moment.

Conditions precedent

These are conditions that you must fulfil before the sale can be completed, such as gaining regulatory approvals or third-party consents. Many years ago, a friend and I offered to buy a group of magazines from a large, publicly traded company. We stressed to the seller that the other buyer they were considering would be unlikely to gain regulatory approval for the purchase due to them being a competitor in the same space. The seller, however, rejected our offer and sold to their competitor without first gaining regulatory approval. Seven months later, as we'd predicted, the competition authority ruled the deal unlawful and so the seller not only had to return their buyer's money but also pay a penalty to cover their legal costs. This is the kind of situation that 'conditions precedent' is designed to prevent.

Completion and closing

Completion date: The day when the transfer of ownership takes place.

Closing procedures: The actions that you and your buyer must take to finalise the sale, such as transferring funds, signing documents and handing over assets.

Post-sale obligations

These mainly take the form of handover arrangements where you lend your experience to help with the transition. This might mean you working as a consultant or an employee of the new business for a set period.

Common sticking points

Because the SPA is such a long and involved document, you may want to direct your attention to the areas that are most likely to provoke difficult conversations between you and your buyer. I'll explain them here.

Restrictive covenants

From your buyer's perspective, restrictive covenants protect their investment by preventing you from doing things that could harm your business after you've sold it, such as setting up in competition or poaching your favourite staff. From your perspective, they inhibit your freedom to do what you like after the sale. If you're not planning on working in a different business in future, they might not matter to you, but if you are, it's an area for discussion.

It helps if you can ensure that you only agree to terms that are as unconstraining as possible. For non-compete clauses, restrictions should be reasonable in scope and duration, and if they're geographically based, they should only focus on the business' actual territory.

For nonsolicitation clauses, there should be clear definitions of the customers, suppliers and employees you're not allowed to approach. The duration and scope should also be reasonable.

Warranties and indemnities

These protect your acquirer from being hit with liabilities that you've not told them about. For instance, suppose a major customer has launched a legal action against your firm which is yet to be resolved, and which you haven't declared as part of the due diligence process. The benefit of warranties and indemnities to your buyer is clear, but from your perspective, they expose you to the risk of being sued in the future. This makes warranties and indemnities critical areas for negotiation.

For warranties, the best way to avoid future problems is to give a full and honest disclosure of all the relevant information during the due diligence process. That way, your buyer can't claim they didn't know anything important. You should also ensure that the warranties only relate to material aspects of your business, and that you negotiate thresholds for what constitutes a material breach. Finally, it's best to agree on time limits for warranty claims, as these reduce the length of your exposure – it's unreasonable for you to be held accountable for problems that arise many years down the line.

For indemnities, it's important that you reduce your risk by defining their scope and ensuring they only cover the necessary areas. Another way to protect your interests is to negotiate limits on the total liability under the indemnities so that, no matter how many claims are made, you're not committed to paying more than a specific amount. Also include provisions for how third-party claims are to be handled, such as that any legitimate claim must be referred in writing to your solicitor within a certain number of days. By pinning down the definitions and timescales, you limit your vulnerability to action being taken against you.

Consultancy and handover agreements

These are important as they smooth the transition to the new ownership, a process that's in both your and your acquirer's interests. At the same time, however, you don't want to be locked into arrangements that are overly onerous for you.

If you're asked to lend your expertise to the new business as a consultant, make sure that you define the scope of work by specifying what tasks, deliverables and time commitments are involved. You also want to agree how much you'll be paid (and in what way), and under what conditions either party can terminate the arrangement early. That way, you have boundaries in place from the start.

For the handover, the agreement should outline how it will be done and what the timeline is for your commitment. It's best to develop a detailed plan, including milestones and deadlines, and to be specific about what support and training you'll provide. At the same time, it's a good idea to build in enough flexibility for dealing with unforeseen challenges during the transition. I'll explore the handover process in detail in the next chapter.

While these sticking points might seem daunting, don't forget that you have your deal team to help. It's your lawyers who'll review the initial agreement and come to you with recommendations about what areas should be negotiated on – you don't have to read the whole thing yourself if you don't want to. And it's they who'll argue your case with your acquirer's legal team, hammering out a deal that works for both parties. Your broker will also remain a key player during this final stage of the sale and can help with negotiating the terms, as well as with co-ordinating the process and keeping it on track. If the lawyers reach a deadlock, for instance, they can talk to both sides and navigate the situation to everyone's satisfaction. There's a hidden benefit to this, which is that if you've agreed to work with your acquirer as a consultant or employee for a year or two after the sale as a condition of your earnout, you don't want to have been embroiled in heated negotiations with them beforehand. It's best to keep yourself at arm's length and let the professionals handle any disagreements.

Finalising the sale

Once the terms have been negotiated and you and your acquirer are in agreement, there are a few important steps to take before it's all over. I've outlined the main ones here.

Satisfying conditions precedent

As you'll remember from earlier, these are conditions that you must fulfil before the sale can be completed, namely gaining regulatory approvals, third-party consents and completing due diligence. Regulatory approvals may involve you submitting filings to governmental authorities and ensuring that you're complying with relevant industry regulations. You'll also need to identify any contracts that require third-party consents for the transfer of ownership, such as framework agreements with government bodies that don't automatically transfer with a change of control or ownership. If you've kept on top of all this throughout the final stages of the process, you'll not delay the finalisation of the deal.

Arranging financing

Your acquirer might be using external finance to fund their purchase, so arranging this is an important element of the sale. If they're taking out a loan, they need to negotiate and finalise the terms. And if they're raising equity, they'll probably have to gain approval from their investors, as well as formalise any shareholder agreements related to it. Much of this will be co-ordinated by your broker, who works closely with your buyer's legal team to make sure that the finance is in place before the sale is complete.

Preparing for closing

Before the ownership of your business is officially transferred, you'll be given a closing checklist by your lawyers that outlines all the tasks and documents required for closing. Some of the tasks relate to the signing and execution of the SPA and other documents, such as deeds of transfer, resignations of directors, and board resolutions. Your job is to assign responsibilities for each action and ensure that everything is completed on time.

After that, it's time for the big moment: the transfer of funds. Your buyer sends the money to their lawyers, who then transfer it to yours. Alternatively, it might go to an escrow agent, who keeps it until agreed conditions are met. In most cases, this signals the completion of the sale, but given that there's many a deal goes through in the early hours of the morning, it might not be until the next day that the monies arrive.

Finally, it's time for the handover of assets. Depending on your business, these can include keys, equipment and stock or inventory, but also intangible assets such as intellectual property and contracts.

You're done!

Completing this final stage of the sale is a complex process, but now that you understand the key elements of the SPA and what to pay most attention to, you should find it easier. Critical to this is preparing for it and making good use of the professionals you're paying to help you, so that you can achieve what you originally set out to do with the sale of your business and enjoy the results. It's certainly time for a celebration.

And yet…despite having signed the contract, your job isn't over. You still have to manage the transition of your business from one owner to another. Depending on the agreement with your acquirer, this can last from anywhere from a few weeks to a couple of years, so it's important that you know what's involved. This is what we'll cover in the next, and final, chapter.

SUMMARY POINTS

- Negotiating and signing the sale and purchase agreement is the final legal step in your business sale journey.
- It's a long and complex document with many areas for discussion, but your legal team is responsible for negotiating it on your behalf.
- It's important to ensure that all the terms are tightly defined and that you understand what you're signing up to.
- You can help the process by making sure that your business documentation is up to date before you reach this stage.

12
The Handover: Twenty-one Secrets To Ensure A Smooth Transition

Reaching the point at which you bank the cheque is no mean feat, but there's more to finalising the sale of your company than signing a contract. You also have to effect the transition to its new owner. There are many tasks involved, some of which may stretch your management and leadership skills to the limit – and this at a time when you're no longer so personally vested in your business (correction: your *buyer's* business). It's also an extra challenge to make the transition work when you're not in charge in the same way as you were before. So, what's in it for you? Why bother?

To begin with, the quality of the transition can affect what you make from the sale. If you have a deferred consideration that's contingent on achieving certain targets, a smooth handover is the best way to reach them. Also, the better the transition goes, the quicker you may be able to leave and pursue your other plans – it's a win-win. But beyond the financial numbers, there's a lot of comfort to be found in knowing that the employees who've worked hard to help you build your firm will be looked after long-term. If you were to abandon ship and leave them to manage the transition on their own, that might not be the case. Finally, it's your buyer who will continue your business' legacy. By maintaining continuity, you preserve value and ensure that both the new owner and your employees are positioned for success.

So, what's involved in the handover? There are two overall elements: transition support, and monitoring and evaluation.

Transition support

This involves giving enough support to your company's new owners to maintain business continuity. It includes onboarding the new owners and their staff through orientation sessions and training programmes, and providing access to all the systems, software and tools they need for running the business. There's also the important element of addressing employee's concerns (communicating with them about the sale and how it affects their roles) and putting in place measures to retain key people, at least for a while.

Monitoring and evaluation

You want the business to carry on thriving. Monitoring and evaluation ensure that you can spot any issues as they arise and do something about them. This involves 'hard' measures, such as creating and monitoring KPIs for business performance, and 'soft' measures, such as gaining feedback from both sets of employees and the new owner.

I mentioned that there's a lot of work to do in the handover period, but there are two things that will help you. One is that you can cover off some of it in advance, while you're agreeing the sale. The other is to be aware that there are some secrets, which I've learned in my many years of buying and selling companies, to achieving a seamless changeover. When I started thinking about these secrets, as I was writing this book, I realised that there are twenty-one in all. It's these that will make up the rest of this chapter.

The twenty-one secrets

1. Start early

Imagine the moment when you announce the sale to the people in your wider business. You'll be bombarded with countless questions, mostly to do with how it affects them. Will they keep their jobs? If so, on what terms? Will they move offices? The list goes on. How will you know what to say if you don't have a transition plan already in place? So often, this situation is mis-handled, resulting in upset and agitated employees, but it doesn't have to be like that. If you start planning well before you complete the sale, it gives you time to work out what to do. In fact, you should be liaising with your buyer about the handover while both sets of lawyers are negotiating the sale and purchase agreement.

Actions:

- Identify the key tasks, with milestones.
- Use them to create an overall transition timeline.

2. Draw up a detailed plan

This should describe every aspect of the transition and incorporate the key areas such as operations, finances, legalities and employees. You can make creating the plan easier for yourself by asking your senior team to document their departmental processes well before the sale. This has the added benefit of adding consistency and stability to your business, because if everyone is following the same processes, mistakes are less likely to happen, and your operations aren't dependent on individual people.

Actions:

- Document all your business processes.
- Create a guide for each department.

- Use the above to create a detailed transition plan with assigned tasks.

3. Talk to your key stakeholders

Liaising early with stakeholders in both businesses increases your chances of gaining their support and addressing their concerns. If your buyer is a large company that has also bought other businesses, it may have its own transition team, so you need to talk to them. In my consultancy, we recently sold two businesses to a large IT firm that's funded by a private equity group. Because it's carried out several acquisitions in the last couple of years and knows how to manage the process, it has its own integration director.

Actions:

- Hold regular meetings with your stakeholders.
- Listen to their feedback and address their concerns.
- Communicate openly about the transition process with everyone as soon as you can.

4. Discover your buyer's needs

In the example above, it would have made little sense for the businesses that we sold to the IT firm to create their own transition plans up front, as their acquirer's transition team would probably have wanted to draft their own. Even if that's not the case with your buyer, it's still important to know their processes before finalising your plan.

As an example, I had a client, Christina, who sold her business to a competitor. Christina used Xero for her financial accounting, but her acquirer used Sage. When she discovered this as part of her exploration into her buyer's needs, she realised that her transition plan needed to cater for her finance team working with a new system. This also had an impact on staff training and retention, as it became clear that her acquirer would have to retain her finance staff for long enough for them to carry out the transition tasks.

Actions:

- Conduct a thorough review of your acquirer's operations so that you can spot the gaps and mismatches with yours.
- Develop plans for bridging those gaps.

5. Develop a communication plan

So much of handling a smooth transition comes down to communication. And to communicate well, you have to know what you want to say, which is where the planning above comes in. But when you have that knowledge, the next step is to decide how, and how often, you'll keep people informed about what's going on.

Actions:

- Create bespoke messages for different audiences.
- Use the best communication channels for those audiences.
- Give regular updates on the transition process so that everyone feels comfortable with what they know.

6. Establish a transition team

The handover process is bigger than you can cope with on your own, so pulling together a team to help you is important. Who you choose depends partly on how comfortable you are with sharing your sale plans in advance of the transaction being completed, but there are certain key people who need to know up front that they'll be asked to do work that's outside their normal scope.

Actions:

- Select your team members based on their experience and seniority.
- Define their roles and responsibilities as members of the team.
- Talk to them regularly to track progress and address any issues.

7. Retain your key employees

Given that your most important staff might be critical to you achieving your earnout, it's important to maintain continuity as much as possible. There are ways to encourage people to stay, such as giving them bonuses for a certain period of commitment. These could be funded by you, your buyer, or both.

Actions:

- Identify the employees and roles that are essential to continuity.
- Offer retention bonuses or other incentives.
- Communicate the benefits of staying with the company.

8. Give training and support

As your people transition into new roles in a different company, they'll require additional training and support. In the example above, of Christina and the new accounting software, for instance, she had to organise training so that her finance team could learn how to use it.

Actions:

- Pinpoint the areas with the highest training needs.
- Develop, or buy in, training programmes that will help the transition.

- Offer ongoing support and coaching.

9. Align cultures and values

The importance of this depends on whether your business is going to be run as a standalone subsidiary of your acquirer, subsumed into it after a set period of time, or subsumed into it immediately. If it's the latter, you'll have some work to do up front to bring your people on board with the new core values, behaviours and culture.

A good example of a cultural shift is the experience of one of my clients, Liam, who recently sold his video graphics business to a large advertising agency that was private-equity owned. While he'd managed to make £1 million profit each year, he's one of the most laid-back people I've ever met, and processes and procedures are certainly not his thing. Many of his staff, for instance, had been working for him for twenty years without an employment contract. Culturally, the shock of becoming part of a £50 million advertising agency is a huge challenge for him, as he navigates the need to document everything and gain signoffs on all expenditure. He's agreed to a year's handover and is already finding it jarring.

Actions:

- Carry out a cultural assessment of your business and that of your acquirer.

- Spot the areas that are aligned and those that could be in conflict.
- Create plans to help bridge the cultural gaps.

10. Integrate systems and processes

Your buyer should have identified areas in which they can leverage economies of scale during their due diligence. This might involve merging both companies' IT or HR systems, for instance, or creating a unified project management process. By liaising with them on this, you can ensure a seamless operation.

Actions:

- Carry out a systems audit to identify the integration needs.
- Create a plan for systems integration.
- For systems that will remain separate, test them to ensure that they're compatible.

11. Manage your customer relationships

After your employees, your customers should be the next stakeholders to know about the sale. In reality, however, this isn't always how it's done. I've seen situations in which, after the internal announcement was made, news spread instantly to customers, and the seller was bombarded with calls from clients who felt disappointed that they'd discovered it through the grapevine. You want your customers to feel as if they're the first people to know the news, not the last. Reassure them that you have a clear plan for how things will work and that, if anything, it will be even better for them under the new ownership. They're bound to have questions: will they have a new point of contact? If so, who? And when will they meet them? You should have answers for all these.

Actions:

- Plan what you'll say to your customers.
- Communicate with them at the first opportunity.
- Reassure them about continuity of service and address their concerns promptly.

12. Manage your supplier relationships

Just as you don't want your customers to feel spooked by the uncertainty of working with a new business, so it's the same for your suppliers. They might have had experience of your acquirer in the past, either positive or negative. They'll also be aware that your acquirer may be looking to make cost savings through consolidating suppliers or by changing their terms. These are all concerns that you should address early on.

Actions:

- Inform your suppliers about the transition as quickly as possible.

- Reassure them about their contracts and tell them how things will work.
- Address any concerns or renegotiate terms if appropriate.

13. Develop a crisis management plan

You can plan to the nth degree, but you still have to cater for the fact that everyone involved in the transition is human. How will you deal with the unexpected? What will you do if an important supplier, for instance, decides that they don't want to work with your acquirer and cancels their latest order? You can't predict every eventuality, but you can work out which are the most obvious and serious risks and put in place strategies to mitigate them.

Actions:

- Identify and rank risks by likelihood and impact.
- Develop a contingency plan for each scenario.
- Train your transition team to handle them.

14. Monitor financial performance

One of the most significant risks when you sell a company is that you become distracted by the long sale process and take your eye off the business' performance. The same goes for the transition, especially in the first few months when everyone is getting used to the new situation and involving themselves in the handover. It's also a classic time for morale to dip, which can have an impact on your financial numbers. If your earnout is contingent on performance, this could be a problem, so you need to be aware of the dangers.

Actions:

- Set up financial KPIs and systems for monitoring them.
- Carry out regular financial reviews.
- Address any concerns without delay.

15. Implement change management principles

It's not only your systems and processes that might change, but also the whole way in which your people approach their work. You need to ensure that everyone has the mental and physical tools they need to navigate the transition.

Actions:

- Communicate your vision and the benefits of the change.
- Give support and resources to help your employees adapt.
- Monitor how the change is progressing and address areas of resistance.

16. Leverage technology

There's a lot of help you can gain from using technology to streamline the transition process.

Actions:

- Use project management software to manage tasks and track deadlines.
- Set up common communication tools between both businesses to aid collaboration.
- Automate routine tasks where you can.

17. Establish clear governance structures

Many years ago, I was a newly appointed CEO of a publishing company; it was a US firm and I was heading up its UK subsidiary. All was going well, but in the run-up to my first Christmas there, I found myself in hot water with the global HR department. The reason? I'd received a gift hamper from a supplier. This, unbeknownst to me, meant that I'd broken the Sarbanes-Oxley Act of 2002, a US federal law that mandates certain practices in financial record-keeping and reporting for companies in an effort to deter corruption. As someone who'd never worked for a US company before, I'd never heard of this law, nor did I know that I was supposed to declare any gift worth over £50. Ironically, I'd already passed the hamper to my PA, but I was still found to have broken the rule.

This is a good example of how you and your employees can fall foul of governance issues in a business that you're not familiar with. It might not be to do with laws but with internal procedures or industry regulations. Whatever it is, you need to know about how things are run and the rules you should keep to.

Actions:

- Decide who's responsible for the various aspects of governance.
- Establish decision-making protocols.
- Hold regular governance meetings to review progress.

18. Focus on long-term planning

Your buyer has long-term plans that you need to be aware of if you're to help them ensure that the transition bears fruit. For Liam, who sold his video graphics business to a large advertising agency as detailed above, this has been yet another adjustment. His sales team has been shocked to discover that the acquiring business carries out its new business development in a significantly different way. Instead of spotting an opportunity and going for it, as Liam's salespeople were used to, they now have to gain two levels of sign-off to ensure that there's no duplication of effort in the wider business. At first, they found this shift really tough, but once they saw how it fitted with the buyer's long-term goals, it made more sense.

Actions:

- Create a long-term, strategic plan that dovetails with that of your acquirer.

- Align your short-term transition activities with their long-term goals.

- Involve the new owners in the planning.

19. Seek professional advice

There's no need to handle the transition alone; there are many professionals you can use, such as accountants, lawyers and specialist consultants, to give you support. Indeed, sometimes it's not a choice but a necessity. Suppose your sales team decides that they don't want to transition to a new company and instead they set up on their own and poach some of your clients in the process. You'd need independent HR and legal advice pretty quickly to cope with the fallout from that.

Actions:

- Identify the areas in which you need professional support.

- Choose experts with the right experience.

- Involve them in your key decisions.

20. Review and adjust your transition plan

This is about continuous improvement. A good plan doesn't stand alone, it needs regular reviewing if it's to carry on working well.

Actions:

- Schedule regular reviews of the plan.
- Gather feedback from stakeholders.
- Adjust the plan based on the feedback and any changes in circumstances.

21. Celebrate success

The transition is hard work, but that's a good reason for celebrating every time you tick off a milestone. Otherwise it's just one long grind, which can lead to a loss of morale and momentum.

Actions:

- Take note of when you've achieved a key milestone or something special.
- Recognise and reward the people involved.
- Tell everyone about the success so as to build confidence that you can all reach the end goal.

While the transition process takes effort – and, just as importantly, a lot of adjustment – it can also be a rewarding time. You're seeing the concrete results of the sale coming through before your eyes, and you're also looking forward to the time when you can move on to the next stage of your life. The one big secret (if I can boil it down to a single piece of advice) is not to take anything for granted: plan, review and communicate. That's how you create the handover that will ensure your business' success for the future.

Conclusion:
The Hidden Benefit

Throughout this book, you may have noticed some themes recurring. It's worth summarising them here, as they encapsulate the underlying approaches that will help you to make the sale that's right for you.

Plan ahead

Deciding to sell your company is best done well before you put it up for sale, because there are so many improvements to make if you're to receive the best possible offer. It's rare to have a business that already fulfils the ten drivers of business value – you need time to put them into place. Whether it's honing your leadership skills so that your people are less dependent on you, documenting your processes so that departments run smoothly and consistently, or adapting your business model so that you bring in more recurring income, these changes can take months or even years to embed.

So often I meet business owners who have the idea to sell up and then forge ahead at full steam straightaway. They're almost always disappointed. Either they fail to sell at all, or they receive offers that are way below what they could have achieved. Your life's work deserves better than that.

Know what you want

You want to sell your business, but beyond that, what do you *really* desire? Is it to pay off your mortgage and travel the world? Exchange a stressful job for the golf course? Or to set up another company and ride the roller coaster all over again? Understanding your motivations not only helps you to prepare yourself for life after the sale, but also for what kind of sale you want. Many of the decisions you make during the sale process depend on you understanding your end goal, such as whether to agree to an earnout or to restrictive covenants that limit what you do afterwards. It's essential to be clear on what's important to you.

Know what your potential buyers want

Just as you have to understand your customers' motivations when you market your brand, so you also need to be clear on what your potential buyers are after when you sell your business. As a group, they want to acquire a company that fufils the ten drivers of business value, but as individuals their needs are more diverse. Seeing your company through the eyes of others is a skill that's worth developing.

Be honest about what needs to change

It wouldn't be surprising if, while reading about the changes you need to make, you were to feel daunted by the scale of the task. And I wouldn't blame you. But unless you're honest with yourself about it, you won't create the sale you want. Of course, you don't have to do everything – rather, it's a question of deciding how much effort you're willing to put in versus what you want to get out. Only you can balance that equation.

Here's where we come to the hidden benefit of learning how to sell your business. Can you see how these four approaches encapsulate much about what makes a business successful in the first place? Forward planning, knowing what you want, understanding what your audience thinks of your business, and being honest about your company's benefits and flaws – all these are essential for any business owner. By getting your business sale-ready and keeping it that way through the transaction and handover, you make it more sustainable and profitable in its own right. What may once have been an owner-reliant company with a high customer turnover and a patchy growth record, now becomes a self-driving, growth-oriented venture with a loyal customer base. It's the very definition of a win-win.

As a coach and consultant who's helped countless people like you to reap the rewards of years of effort by selling their business, I know what a difference the perfect exit can make. When you have the time and money to embark on your next adventure because you've done it right, all the hard work will have been worthwhile. I'd like to wish you the best of luck, but being honest, I don't think that luck should come into it. It's knowledge and action that are the keys, and with this book you're equipped with both. You have your roadmap, so I encourage you to get yourself and your company ready for sale right now, and start preparing to achieve the transaction that will set you up for years to come. Here's to your future.

Acknowledgements

As I reflect on the journey that's led to the completion of this book, I'm filled with immense gratitude for the individuals and organisations who contributed to its creation, as well as to the ideas and strategies it discusses.

First and foremost, I want to extend my heartfelt thanks to my clients, past and present. You are the true driving force behind everything I do. Your trust, collaboration and willingness to embark on new ventures have pushed me and the team at Chalkhill Blue to innovate and consistently strive for excellence. Without your confidence in our capabilities and vision, this book would not exist. It's a real privilege to be able to help and support you. Your businesses are the canvas upon which we apply our expertise, and the results we achieve together are the foundation for much of what is shared in these pages. Your challenges, aspirations and successes continue to inspire us to evolve and push boundaries.

To the incredible people in my team, I owe a debt of gratitude that can't be easily expressed. Each of you brings a unique set of skills, perspectives and passion that makes the work I do not only possible, but meaningful. Your tireless dedication and commitment to our shared goals are evident in every project we take on. You have been my support system, my sounding board, and my partners. This book reflects not just my thoughts and experiences, but the collective wisdom, insights and relentless pursuit of excellence that each of you embodies. Thank you for your hard work, perseverance and belief in what we are building together.

A special thank you is due to our strategic partners. This book stresses the importance of recognised experts within any deal team, and you all play a pivotal role in helping our clients to achieve their exit goals, and in helping us to expand our reach, innovate our offerings and scale our impact. Through collaborative projects, shared insights, or simply providing the support we needed to grow, you've been indispensable allies. Your expertise, commitment and values have not only enriched our business but have helped to shape the content and perspectives shared within these pages. We look forward to continuing to strengthen these relationships and to create even more impactful outcomes together in the future.

Lastly, I would also like to thank Ginny Carter, whose talent and skill have been instrumental in transforming my ideas into a clear, compelling narrative. Writing a book is no small feat, and your ability to take complex thoughts and distil them into engaging and accessible prose is truly remarkable. Thank you for capturing my voice and vision with such clarity and precision.

Thank you to everyone who has been part of this journey. This book is as much yours as it is mine.

The Author

During his thirty years in business, Chris Spratling has been an entrepreneur, a strategic mergers and acquisitions professional, and a trusted business coach. As the owner, buyer and seller of multiple seven-figure businesses himself, he has first-hand experience of navigating the challenges that come with entrepreneurship. His many successful ventures show his ability to identify market opportunities, drive growth, and achieve substantial financial success. This practical experience forms the bedrock of his knowledge when it comes to selling a business.

Chris' history is diverse. Throughout his career, he's

worked across numerous industry sectors and companies of differing scales ranging from PLCs to small- and medium-sized businesses, and equally many family-owned businesses – both in the UK and internationally. This gives him a broad-based perspective on the challenges and opportunities faced by different types of companies, and it's his ability to tailor his approach to the specific needs of each client that's made him a sought-after advisor.

Fundamental to his success is his ability to get to the heart of an issue and devise effective solutions. This, combined with his deep understanding of market dynamics and valuation principles, is what's made him a leading authority on business sales. He has a relentless drive for excellence and a commitment to helping people achieve their business goals.

Chris' entrepreneurial experience is complemented by his role as founder of Chalkhill Blue Limited, a leading business coaching and consulting practice. The firm specialises in helping business owners to scale their companies' operations, and in many cases to achieve successful exits. Under his guidance, the firm has developed a robust, value-oriented growth methodology that combines strategic insight with practical advice, and has enabled hundreds of entrepreneurs to maximise their business value and prepare for the successful exits that they've always dreamed of.

Beyond his coaching business, Chris is a well-known speaker who regularly shares his insights at industry conferences and events. At these, he educates business owners on the best practices for scaling and selling their businesses. His ability to articulate complex concepts in an engaging and accessible way has made him a favourite with audiences, and inspires them to exit in a way that's right for them.

If you'd like to bring Chris' strategic vision, hands-on experience and wealth of knowledge to your own business sale, please visit www.chalkhillblue.org.